HIGHLAND SETTLER

North River Bridge—a typical Highland settlement in Cape Breton Island, Nova Scotia. Here in the Presbyterian Church (centre) precentors can still lead the singing of the psalms in Gaelic. (Nova Scotia Bureau of Information Photograph)

HIGHLAND SETTLER

*A Portrait of the Scottish
Gael in Nova Scotia*

BY CHARLES W. DUNN

UNIVERSITY OF TORONTO PRESS: 1953

3522

TO MY WIFE

An teid thu leam, a ribhinn og,
A null gu tir nam beanntan?

Preface

~~~~~~

BETWEEN the end of the eighteenth and the middle of the nineteenth century, many of the Gaelic-speaking inhabitants of the
Highlands and Western Islands emigrated from Scotland to
North America. In this book I have attempted to record the
experience of the settlers and their descendants and to describe
the effects of emigration upon their folk-culture.[1] My investi-
gations naturally do not purport to be exhaustive; they have
been restricted principally to those settlers and descendants who
made their homes in Nova Scotia, in the eastern Maritimes of
Canada.

My own interest in the topic can be partly explained by the
fact that I was born in Scotland. But, though I spent my childhood there, I did not at that time acquire Gaelic. Later, however,
as a graduate student in the English Department at Harvard
(1938-41), I studied Celtic language and literature under Pro-
fessor Fred Norris Robinson and folklore under Professors Bart-
lett Jere Whiting and Kenneth Jackson, and it was then that I
decided to undertake an investigation of Gaelic folk-culture.

My information was collected in two ways. I consulted all the
published sources available to me, such as local histories, Gaelic
song-books, broadsides, pamphlets, and periodicals.[2] And I recorded at first hand in Nova Scotia the oral traditions and observed the folkways of the Gaelic-speaking descendants of the
Highland settlers.

Exaggerated claims have been made concerning the extent to
which the Gaelic language has survived in North America. For
instance, a somewhat irresponsible encyclopaedia published in
1911 suggests that the number of Gaelic-speaking people in the
United States was then, at a "conservative estimate," "not less

than 1,000,000." The least that can be said is that the editor was a Scot and that his surmise is unverifiable. But this much we do know. According to the dispassionate figures of the Canadian census of 1941, in Cape Breton Island alone—the most Gaelic part of Nova Scotia—there were approximately 10,000 people who listed Gaelic as their mother tongue.[3] This number may seem small compared to the 137,000 Gaelic speakers, approximately, enumerated in the 1931 census of Scotland, but it serves to indicate the persistency with which Gaelic culture has, for over a century, resisted the neutralizing effects of the New World environment.

It was to Cape Breton that my wife and I first went in the summer of 1941, when Harvard granted me a Dexter Traveling Scholarship. And later, when the Rockefeller Foundation granted me a Fellowship in the Humanities for the academic year 1942-3, we travelled through various parts of Nova Scotia but once again lived for the most part in the rural farming and fishing settlements of Cape Breton.

I am thus indebted to the hospitality, kindness, and patience of many informants—professors, teachers, librarians, doctors, priests, nuns, ministers, store-keepers, farmers, fishermen, miners, housewives, and even children—so many, in fact, that it would be impracticable to mention them all by name. But in what follows I have embodied many of their comments, either verbatim or in substance, so that in a sense they are the authors of this book; and in the appended notes I have attempted to acknowledge these sources of information, except in a few cases where I have felt that anonymity might be preferred by the informant.

Publication of the book has been assisted by the Humanities Research Council of Canada and the Publication Fund of the University of Toronto Press.

Two maps, drawn by Mrs. W. C. Wonders of the Geography Department of the University of Toronto, indicate the location of most of the places, either large or small, in Scotland and Nova Scotia referred to in the text.

The map of Scotland is based upon the clan maps in the first volume of David Stewart's *Sketches of the Character of the Highlanders of Scotland* (2nd ed., Edinburgh, 1822) and in T. B.

Johnston and James A. Robertson's *Historical Geography of the Clans of Scotland* (Edinburgh, 1899), and upon the linguistic map in E. G. Ravenstein's "On the Celtic Languages," *Journal of the Statistical Society*, vol. 42 (London, 1879), p. 592. The traditional Highland Line marked on this map does not correspond precisely to any one physiographic division, but it is significant in its distinction between the areas of Gaelic and of Lowland Scottish culture.

The map of Nova Scotia is based on the geological maps of Cape Breton Island (one inch to the mile) published by Hugh Fletcher to accompany the Canadian Geological Survey's *Reports of Progress* for 1875-6, 1876-7, and 1882-4 and the similar maps of the adjoining mainland by Hugh Fletcher and E. R. Faribault published in the Survey's *Annual Report* (*New Series*), vol. 2 (1887). These maps are of especial value because they record place-names of remote settlements more adequately than the standard topographic maps and even indicate the names of some householders, Highlands settlements being thus signalized by the presence of Chisholms, Gillises, MacDonalds, MacKinnons, MacLeans, MacLeods, and the like. Discrepancies between varying forms and spellings of place-names have been resolved as far as possible in favour of local usage.

It is to be hoped that the tourists who are impressed by the rich variety of the scenery in Cape Breton will be assisted by this book to appreciate something of the intangible yet vigorous heritage of folk-culture still preserved by the descendants of the Highland settlers amid the equally rich variety of Nova Scotia's population. From the Canadian maritimes to Florida, farmers in overalls and fishermen in rubber boots now look very much the same externally, but even today to those of Highland origin in Nova Scotia the familiar words of the *Canadian Boat Song* still apply most aptly:

> From the lone shieling of the misty island
> Mountains divide us, and the waste of seas—
> Yet still the blood is strong, the heart is Highland,
> And we in dreams behold the Hebrides.

C. W. D.

University of Toronto
October, 1952

Contents

HIGHLAND SETTLER

1

~~~~~~

The Old Home

SCOTLAND is traditionally divided into two geographical regions, one comprising the Highlands and Western Islands, mountainous and bare, and the other the Lowlands, level and populous. These areas are often separated on maps by means of a division labelled "The Highland Line"; but maps do not undertake to explain the difference between the inhabitants of the two sections, between the Highlander and the Lowlander. Here the difference is not a tangible one of rocks and rivers but an elusive distinction of human customs and traditions. It is obviously not sufficient, then, to explain the Highlander by saying that he comes from the Highlands. To make a fair judgment of his way of life and his character, we must understand something of his environment and heredity.

The Highlander is descended from the Gaelic branch of the widespread family of Celts who in prehistoric times swept westward across Europe.[1] At an early date Gaelic-speaking emigrants from the Continent settled in Ireland, and descendants of the Irish Gaels later landed in the west of Scotland, at least fourteen hundred years ago. Here, combining the missionary activities of Christians with the military conquest of invaders, they established their own Gaelic culture. They introduced to the country their own monastic system, their own clan organization and legal code, their own forms of art, and their own Gaelic language, literature, and music.[2] They rapidly extended their power over the greater part of Scotland, so that in the eleventh century during the unhappy reigns of the two Scottish kings immortalized by Shakespeare, Duncan and Macbeth, the official language of the court was Gaelic. But history brought reverses to the power of the Gaels and gradually

3

narrowed down their sphere of influence to the present limits of the Highland Line. Today only a small part of their distinguishing heritage survives in Scotland. Their monasteries gave way to the more widespread church system of Britain, their clan organization and legal code submitted to the rule of the Lowlander, and their art lost its vigour; but a memory of the old Gaelic music and literature lingers among the Highlanders, and the language, although altered, survives to the present day as Scottish Gaelic, the mother tongue of the people of the Highlands and Islands, though now the majority of them can also speak English.

In Scottish residence the Lowlanders are slightly more recent than the Highlanders. Their forefathers were English-speaking people, the Angles of Northumberland, who worked their way northward from England into the eastern section of Scotland.[3] Their language (including the native "broad Scots" dialects, familiarly represented by the stage Scotsman with his "burr," and the more "cultivated" standard English, heard particularly in Lowland cities) now greatly preponderates over Gaelic. Their present way of life, that of the majority of the population of Scotland, resembles that of the English to the south of them.

This historical division is, culturally, not a simple one. Although it is true to say that the Highlander is descended from the Gael, and the Lowlander from the Angle, we must remember that Scotland's total population was not built up from these two constituents alone. Scotland lies far west from the Garden of Eden, and her shores and valleys may not seem to be such as would offer the promise of a luxuriant paradise to the wanderer, but, during her long history, many groups of migrants have sought out her soil. Before the Gaels arrived from Ireland, the Picts were settled in the east of Scotland, and the Britons on the southwest, and other, lesser tribes were scattered through the land.[4] After the settlement of the Gaels and of the Angles, Norse and Danish seafarers wrested dwelling space for themselves from the inhabitants;[5] and Normans, following up their conquest of England in 1066, filtered peaceably into the land from the south.[6] But despite the complexity of the population, the Gaels have in general succeeded in predominating over one part

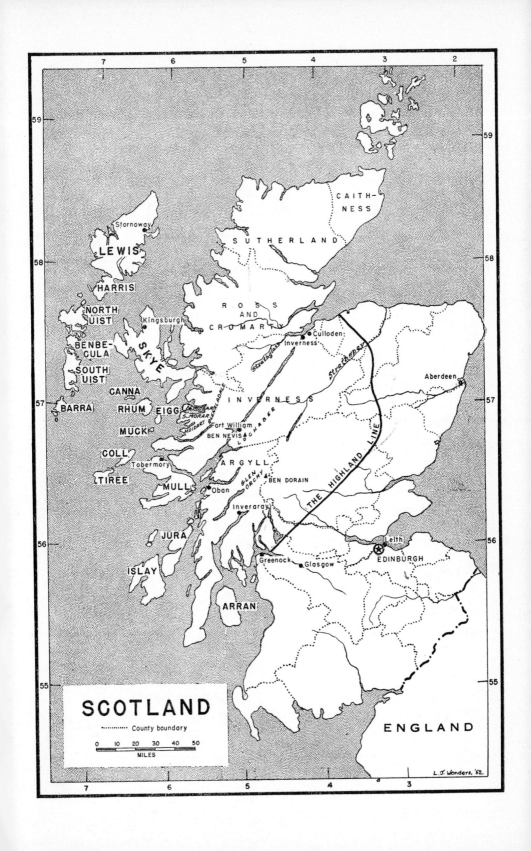

SCOTLAND

----------- County boundary

0 10 20 30 40 50
MILES

L.J.Wonders, '52

of Scotland, while the Angles have predominated over the other, so that the twofold division has been recognized from an early date. Thus about the year 1250 an encyclopaedist, Bartholomew the Englishman by name, as an outsider differentiates only two groups within Scotland: the one, those who have been mellowed by English ways, and the other, the "wild Scots" ("silvestres Scoti," as he calls them in the original Latin) who glory in following the manner of their forefathers both "in dress, in language, in way of life, and in other habits."[7] Some three centuries later John Major, a native-born Scot, separates the two groups still more precisely: ". . . just as there are two languages, so also there are two different ways of life among the Scots; for some of them are born in the northern forests and mountains, and these we call Highlanders; while the others we call Lowlanders. Outsiders call the first group wild (*silvestres*) Scots, and the second group, householding (*domestici*) Scots."[8]

History, then, explains the origin of the Highland group, but it does not explain the character of the Highland people; it does not tell us, for instance, why they were labelled "wild Scots" by Bartholomew the Englishman and by John Major's "outsiders." Such manifestations of the Highlander's character must be interpreted in the light not merely of his ancestry but also of his environment. According to the geographers, the terrain of the Highlands is characterized by its exceptional "relief," its violent inequality.[9] Because of this characteristic of his country, the Highlander will always find himself living close to the face of a mountain. He need not, of course, live *on* a mountain, and in most cases he does not. All the important centres of population within his territory, such as Inverness and Fort William and Oban on the mainland, and Stornoway and Tobermory on the Western Islands, are located either close to the sea, or on waterways little higher than sea level. But the Highlander need never look far to see the steep slopes peculiar to a country of abrupt relief. At Tobermory, for instance, or at any other point along the thirty-mile length of Mull, the islander lives in the shadow of Ben More, a mountain more than 3,100 feet in height. And from Fort William, by a walk of only seven miles the traveller can reach the summit of Ben Nevis, the highest mountain in the

British Isles, some 4,400 feet above sea level.[10] This mountainous environment explains much of the Highlander's character and way of life. Knowing this setting, we can understand why Samuel Johnson wrote after his tour of the Highlands in 1773: "To the southern inhabitants of Scotland the state of the mountains and the islands is equally unknown with that of Borneo or Sumatra; of both they have only heard a little and guess the rest."[11] Presumably Scotland's southern inhabitants were actually more curious about the Highland people than about the people of Borneo or Sumatra, but geography's formidable barriers of mountain, river, and sea made the Highlander's homeland discouragingly inaccessible.

Geographical impediments to transportation and communication have noticeably affected the Highlander's well-being. Though they may have produced an admirable spirit of independence in the Highland character, they have unquestionably thwarted the development of unity among the many isolated groups of people. One instance of the sectionalism within the Highlands is offered by the local dialects of the Gaelic language. So slight has been the intercommunication between the various Highland communities that each preserves its own clearly recognizable dialect. The Barra man, the Lochaber man, the Lewis man, the Skye man—each speaks his own variety of Gaelic and will stoutly defend its peculiarities, its local terms, its intonation. Unlike those who live in countries where travel is unimpeded, the Gaels have developed no accepted standard of speech to which educated classes conform. But more damaging by far than variations in dialect have been the mutual suspicion, rivalry, and warfare between the various groups within the narrow confines of the country. The environment that cultivated independence among the people seems to have bred contentiousness proportionally. Hence it is that the early writers speak of the Highlanders as the "wild Scots," and popular histories such as Sir Walter Scott's *Tales of a Grandfather* inevitably depict the life of the clansman as one of perpetual feud and slaughter.

Another serious shortcoming of the Highlander's environment has been its inadequacy to support a farming population

of any great size. Cultivation in a country so precipitous as
the Highlands must necessarily be limited to the sparse, scattered areas of comparatively level land lying along river valleys
and the lower fringes of mountains. More abrupt slopes defy any
efforts at tillage and do not even offer pasture adequate for
live-stock. As a result the location of settlements within the
Highlands has been determined by the whims of geology, and
farms are dotted at random along the rare stretches of level
ground often considerably separated from one another, hemmed
in on one side by the immensity of the mountains and on the
other by the fury of the sea.

It would be a mistake, however, to exaggerate the difficulties
of the Highlands. Environmental hardships are to some extent
relative, and their effect upon man depends upon his adaptive-
ness. The sea, rivers, and lochs provided the Highlander with
fish; the mountains sheltered game, the enjoyment of which, to
be sure, was liable to restriction by the landed proprietors; the
undrained bogs supplied peat for fuel; and the terrain provided
freestone for building. The subjective judgment of outside
observers may be misleading. The squat, windowless, thatch-
covered "black houses" still to be seen on the island of Lewis,
for instance, have been called picturesque by romanticists in the
nineteenth century and sordid by social reformers in the
twentieth, but the geographer reminds us that the inhabitants
have ingeniously utilized the extremely limited selection of
building materials available on the island and have suited the
design of their dwellings to the exigencies of the climate.[12]

Certainly Gaelic poets reveal no dislike for their native
surroundings. In fact, during the eighteenth century they produced a considerable body of nature poetry, at the very time
when English travellers customarily expressed a polite horror at
the violence of Highland scenery. Daniel Defoe, for instance,
who had so enthusiastically glorified life on a desert island,
returned from his tour of Great Britain (1727) with the undis-
guised feeling that to live in the mountains of Scotland was a
fate far worse than shipwreck. He describes the territory south
of Lochaber as "a frightful country, full of hideous desert mountains, and unpassable except to the Highlanders who possess

the precipices."[13] Yet while Defoe's guide-book was circulating in England, a Gaelic poet was growing up in the heart of the defamed area quite unconscious of its hideousness. In two of his best-known poems, *The Praise of Ben Dorain* and *A Last Farewell to the Mountains*,[14] this bard, Duncan Ban MacIntyre of Glen Orchy, immortalized the rugged slopes of Ben Dorain, the mountain which towers above his birth-place, rising more than 3,500 feet above sea level.

> Bha mi 'n de 'm Beinn-Dorain,
> 'S 'n a coir cha robh mi aineolach.
> Chunna' mi na gleanntan
> 'S na beanntaichean a b' aithne dhomh.
> B' e sin an sealladh eibhinn
> 'Bhith 'g imeachd air na sleibhtean
> Nuair bhiodh a' ghrian ag eiridh,
> 'S a bhiodh na feidh a' langanaich.
>
> 'S togarrach a dh' fhalbhainn
> Gu sealgaireachd nam bealaichean,
> Dol mach a dhireadh garbhlaich,
> 'S gu'm b' anmoch tighinn gu baile mi.
> An t-uisge glan 's am faileadh
> Th' air mullach nam beann arda
> Chuidich e gu fas mi,
> 'S e rinn dhomh slaint' us fallaineachd.

Yesterday I was on Ben Dorain, and in her presence I felt myself no stranger, for I saw the glens and mountains which I used to know. There you'll find a view heart-warming as you wander over the hillsides when the sun is rising and the stags are bellowing.

Jauntily I used to set out stalking in the passes, climbing up the moorland, and returning late to the homestead. The pure water and the scent on the crest of the tall mountains helped to build me up and gave me health and vigour.

The bards were connoisseurs of the beauties of crag and cliff and possessed in their mother tongue a rich vocabulary descriptive of the varied types of hills and knolls, peaks and mountains, which every day they saw around them. *Aonach, bac, beinn, binnean, braighe, carn, cnoc, coire, creag, cruach, fireach, leathad, mam, monadh, sgorr, sliabh, slios, stuc, tolm, torr* —such specialized and almost untranslatable terms offer a sample of the words at their disposal.

The Highlanders show a correspondingly enthusiastic appreciation for the sea, even though those who ventured their lives on the angry waters of the Atlantic recognized its menace. Alexander MacDonald warns us in ominous language:

> Gur neo-aoigheil turus-Faoilthich
> Ged bhiodh na daoine tabhachdach,
>
> An fhairge molach, bronnach, torach,
> Giobach, corrach, rapalach.[15]

It's unpleasant to sail at the winter's end, no matter how hardy the crew, when the ocean is stormy, swelling, overbrimming, rough, impassioned, and roaring.

But Kenneth MacKenzie, nothing daunted, sings lustily in a song honouring his sail-boat:

> 'S i mo cheisd an capull grinn,
> Rachadh leinn air an aiseag,
> 'S taobh an fhuaraidh fos a cinn,
> 'S muir ri slinn taobh an fhasgaidh.
>
> Nuair a chuirte i air a doigh
> 'S a cuid seol ris na racan,
> Chuirte a mach an t-aodach sgeoid—
> Siud a sron ris an ascaoin.[16]

She's my darling, the handsome steed, that would take us on our journey with her windward side high, and her leeward in sea to the gunwale.

When she was trimmed, with her sails run up and her canvas set out on the sheet, then hers was the prow for bad weather.

And Donald MacKechnie finds companionship in the restless sea:

> Tha 'n cuan dhomhsa mar fhear-eolais
> Tighinn am chomhdhail air an traigh,
> Fiamh a' ghair' air aodann preasach,
> 'S a thuinn bheaga cur orm failt'.[17]

For me the ocean is like a friend as it comes up to meet me on the shore with the tinge of a smile on its wrinkled face, and its lapping wavelets greeting me.

Despite the difficulties of his environment, the Highlander loved his native land, and, where visitors saw only the unfriendly face of Nature, he could find inspiration.

2

Parting

THE EIGHTEENTH CENTURY marks a significant change in the destiny of the Highlanders. In 1715 they rose against the Hanoverian George I, and attempted to place James, the Old Pretender, upon the throne. Although this attempt was defeated, in 1745 they rose against George II in support of the claims advanced by the Pretender's son, Charles Edward ("Bonnie Prince Charlie"). But at Culloden in 1746 the Highland Jacobites were vanquished. The hereditary power of their chieftains was destroyed, and that section of Scotland which had once sheltered independent bands of fighting men was converted into a quiet countryside, the home of powerless farmers and fishermen. Military roads were constructed through their midst, and the central government at last acquired what it long had aimed at, namely a unified control over the entire country. The change, which brought peace to the nation, brought indignity to the Highlanders. Samuel Johnson was touched by what he saw of the once warlike people during his travels through the Highlands and Islands some thirty years after their last unsuccessful rebellion: "The clans retain little now of their original character; their ferocity of temper is softened, their military ardour is extinguished, their dignity of independence is depressed, their contempt of government subdued, and their reverence for chiefs abated. Of what they had before the late conquest of their country, there remain only their language and their poverty."[1]

Until the power of the clans was broken, each chief had encouraged men to settle within his own domain so that he could call out a powerful battle-force in time of feud or war. But when feuds were forbidden by the central authorities and civil war within the country was unlikely, the chieftain's many retainers were no longer a source of strength but an economic embarrass-

11

ment.[2] It is not surprising, therefore, that the eighteenth century saw the beginning of what Samuel Johnson called an "epidemical fury of emigration"[3] to North America.

As the emigration continued during the following hundred and more years after the defeat in 1746, the several forces[4] producing the exodus from the Highlands varied in nature and in relative importance; but basically people left their homeland either because economic pressure drove them out, or because the prospects of the New World lured them away.

The decline in warfare in the latter part of the eighteenth century and the introduction of innoculation combined to produce a decrease in the death rate among the Highland population. At the same time the adoption of the potato by the Highland farmer enabled him to feed a larger family than his poorly supplied forefather had been able to do. But, although potatoes may build a healthy family, they do not provide a livelihood for it, and the resources of the unexuberant homeland became overtaxed.

Scarcity of money also troubled the Highlander. When the new landlords replaced the traditional chieftains, the price of land rose so excessively that the small tenant farmer saw little prospect of raising enough on his farm to pay his annual rent. And at the beginning of the nineteenth century the kelp industry, which had supplied Britain with alkali and provided the inhabitants of the Western Isles with a means of livelihood, collapsed when barilla, a foreign substitute, cornered the market. In such circumstances the poorer class among the Highlanders had the choice of emigrating or starving.

In some parts of the Highlands landlords found that, because of rising prices in the wool market, they could derive more revenue from their property by raising sheep on it than by renting it out, and they therefore evicted their unprofitable farmer-tenants. When these clearances became notorious, public opinion was shocked. In a somewhat unpoetical stanza the anonymous author of the *Canadian Boat Song* (published in 1829) cried:

> When the bold kindred, in the time long-vanish'd,
> Conquer'd the soil and fortified the keep,

No seer foretold the children would be banish'd,
That a degenerate lord might boast his sheep.[5]

Intelligent observers of the general process of depopulation
in the Highlands were alarmed at the loss of such fine stock
from Britain, but no one succeeded in solving the problem of
the excess population, and so the stream of migration continued.

Somewhat happier was the fate of those who did not leave
the Highlands entirely unwillingly but had some reason to
prefer the New World. Among these were the many active
Jacobite sympathizers who felt that after the collapse of Bonnie
Prince Charlie's cause in 1746 they would be less circumscribed
by political enemies in America than in Scotland. Of these,
certainly the most colourful was Allan MacDonald of Kings-
burgh, whose dramatic personal history[6] has been unduly
obscured by the romance and fame attached to his wife, Flora
MacDonald, who helped the defeated Young Pretender to
escape from Scotland. Because of political and financial em-
barrassment Captain Allan and his wife found it advisable to
leave Scotland in 1773 and seek their fortune in North Carolina.
Arriving on the eve of the American Revolution, by a strange
irony Captain Allan supported the cause of King George III,
was captured by the colonists, imprisoned in Virginia, and later
released. Disappointed in the freedom which they had hoped to
enjoy in the New World, the Captain and Flora eventually
found their way back to Scotland and spent their last days there.

Not all political refugees suffered in this manner, however.
John MacDonald, the laird of Glenaladale, for instance, sold his
estate in Scotland in 1772 and brought out 250 followers with
him to Prince Edward Island; they settled peacefully on the
island, gained their independence, and prospered; in less than a
hundred years the descendants of the original settlers numbered
3,000.[7]

Other Highlanders came to the New World because they
longed to find religious freedom. In Scotland the Reformation,
which turned so many of the inhabitants from the Catholic
faith to the Protestant, did not affect the entire country, and
particularly in some districts of the Highlands and Islands the
people continued unaltered in their old faith. Because of the

support which they had given to the defeated cause of Bonnie
Prince Charlie, they were subjected by the Protestant victors[8]
to a persecution which the numerous Catholics of Highland
descent in the New World today cite as the cause of their forefathers' exodus from Scotland. At a religious celebration in 1915
at Christmas Island, a Highland settlement in Cape Breton,
Father MacAdam[9]—himself descended from the Catholic
refugees—in a Gaelic address reminded his audience of the
distressing events:

> . . . thainig Prionnsa Tearlach a' chruaidh-fhortain air tir am
> Muideart. Dh' eirich na Caitleacaich leis mar aon dhuine. Chath iad
> gu treun 'n a aobhar. . . . Ach, mo thruaigh, bha Sasunn tuille 's
> beartach; bha saighdearan Shasunn tuille 's lionmhor air an son.
> Agus air raon Chuil-lodair, fuar us fann us sgith, gun urram aon
> do cheile, thuit iad 'n an ciadan roimh ghunnaichean mora nan
> Deasach. . . .
> Agus ma bha geur-leanmhainn air na Caitleacaich roimhe sin,
> cha robh a bhith beo idir aca 'n a deigh. . . . Ach an roghainn air
> an creideimh aicheadh dh' fhag na h-aidmheilich threuna tir an
> gaoil; liubhair iad seachad an cuid de'n t-saoghail; agus thog iad leo
> am mnathan 's an leanaban tarsuinn air a' chuan gu dachaidhean
> ura a dheanamh dhaibh fhein ann na coilltean gruamach America.
> 'S doirbh dhuinne 'thuigsinn an amhghair a dh' fhulaing iad, ach
> bha fearann ri fhaotainn am pailteas; bha iasg anns an linne agus
> sealg anns na beannaibh; agus bha iad saor gu aoradh a thoirt do
> Dhia mar a thug an aithrichean fad corr us da-chiad-diag bliadhna
> gun uachdaran aig ceann an rathaid gus am fuadach bho thaigh
> Dhe.[10]

> . . . the unfortunate Prince Charlie landed at Moidart. The Catho-
> lics rose with him as one man. They fought heroically in his cause. . . .
> But, alas, England was too wealthy; the English soldiers were too
> numerous for them. And on Culloden moor, cold, famished, weary,
> and leaderless, they fell in hundreds before the cannons of the
> Southerners. . . .
> And, if the Catholics were persecuted before then, thereafter they
> were scarcely allowed to live. . . . But rather than forsake their
> faith the heroic confessors left the land of their love; they parted
> with their worldly goods; and they took their wives and children
> with them across the ocean to make new homes for themselves in
> the melancholy forests of America.
> We can scarcely conceive the sufferings which they endured, but
> land was plentiful; there were fish in the waters and game on the
> mountains; and they were free to worship God in the way that their
> fathers had for more than twelve hundred years, without any land-
> lord standing at the cross-road to drive them away from the house
> of God.

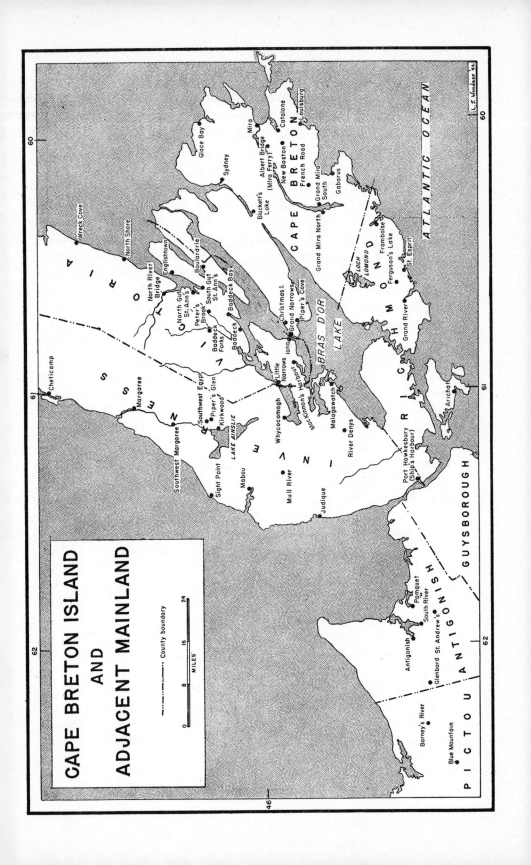

CAPE BRETON ISLAND
AND
ADJACENT MAINLAND

------- County boundary

MILES

0   8   16   24

ATLANTIC OCEAN

L. J. Wanders '63

60

60

VICTORIA

Wreck Cove

North Shore

Cheticamp

61

Margaree

Southwest Margaree

INVERNESS

Englishtown
North River Bridge
Boularderie
North Gut St. Ann's
South Gut St. Ann's
Baddeck Bay
Peter's Brook
Baddeck
Baddeck Forks

Glace Bay

Sydney

Blackett's Lake
Albert Bridge (Mira Ferry)
New Boston
French Road
Grand Mira North
Grand Mira South
Gabarus

Mira
Catalone
Louisburg

CAPE BRETON

Christmas I.
Grand Narrows
Iona
Piper's Cove

BRAS D'OR LAKE

LOCH LOMOND

Framboise
Ferguson's Lake
St. Esprit

RICHMOND

Grand River

Southwest Egypt
Piper's Glen
Kirkwood
LAKE AINSLIE

Little Narrows
MacKinnon's Harbour
Whycocomagh

Iona

Malagawatch
River Denys

Sight Point
Mabou
Mull River

Judique

Port Hawkesbury (Ship's Harbour)

Arichat

61

Pomquet
South River
Glenbard St. Andrew's

Antigonish

ANTIGONISH

GUYSBOROUGH

Barney's River

Blue Mountain

PICTOU

62

62

46

Whether the Highlander emigrated from economic necessity or from personal choice, he certainly could not have relished parting from the homeland which he loved; yet even the most wretched emigrant, as he embarked on the voyage, must have nourished some ray of hope in the possibilities of the new and unexploited land of the New World. Behind the whole restless movement away from the Highlands lay more than the breaking down of the old order, more than the impersonal operation of economic principles. The emigrants may be said to have been impelled by democratic idealism, providing we recognize the ideals as eminently practical. Those whose only home had been a one-roomed stone cottage and whose only farm had been a rented patch of stony ground dreamed of broad, fertile fields; those who had been subjected to the caprice of a heartless land-lord looked forward to land of their own; those who had lived in fear of political enemies yearned for personal liberty; those who had suffered persecution for their religious faith thirsted for freedom of worship. The same aspirations which fired the revolutionary spirit of the common man in the American colonies and in France were beginning to awaken the Highlander. The apostles of democracy, many of them obscure, to be sure, were at work in the Highlands. One commentator reports in 1806 that self-appointed preachers, travelling among the High-landers on the banks of the Caledonian Canal, were teaching that all men are equal and that no man should be a slave to work, and recommending emigration as a cure for social ills.[11] Another writer, conservatively opposed to any change in the Highlands, complains a few years later that some of the High-landers feel that they are oppressed and have therefore (to quote his own words) "sought consolaticn in the doctrines of ignorant and fanatical spiritual guides."[12] Such teaching, whether it seemed at the time desirable or undesirable to the disinterested observer, probably met with a ready response among the High-landers.

The spirit of independence among the emigrants is amply illustrated by the records of individual pioneers, such as Hector mac Sheumais MacNeil of Barra,[13] who was born in the latter part of the eighteenth century. After marriage he went to the

Lowlands in search of employment and found work at Glasgow
in the quarries at a wage of sixpence per day. He was satisfied,
but the laird of Barra wished him to take over a farm on the
island and lured him back with an enticing offer. All went well
until one day the laird had visitors and found that he had no
provisions for them in his larder. He sent a servant to Hector's
croft to bring back whatever he could find there; the servant
returned to his master with some of Hector's best poultry, taken
without the knowledge or permission of the owner. When
Hector discovered how he had been raided, he complained
bitterly, and the year 1802 saw him sailing out to Canada. He
landed in Pictou and a year later settled at Grand Narrows,
Cape Breton, and contentedly reared his family in a land where
his private property could not be molested.

A similar story is told about a certain Peter MacKellar,[14] who
was born in Inveraray in the Highlands of Scotland. After he
married, he was employed as a farm-hand by a colonel whose
wife was an excessively exacting mistress. One day Peter was
ploughing; a friend of his came up to him with some message and
interrupted the work for a few minutes. Peter's mistress saw her
workman standing idle in the field and shouted an ill-natured
reproach at him. With the quick anger characteristic of a Gael,
Peter did not return to his task but unyoked the horses, put
them back in the stable, and went home. He said to his wife:
"If there's any place under the sun where I can be free from the
humiliating bondage of this wretched employment, I'll go there."
(Ma tha aite fo'n ghrein anns an urrainn domh a bhith saor o
chuing taireil an dubhsheirbhis, theid mi 'n sin.) "We'll go
together," said his sympathetic wife. And, within that same
year (1817), they were settled on a farm of their own in Ontario.
Here Peter's independence profited not only himself but also his
son, who had been born the year before his family left Scotland;
for, by the time Archie MacKellar, the son of the maltreated
farm-hand, was forty years of age, he had become a member of
the Legislative Assembly of Upper Canada.

No enumeration of the causes of emigration should obscure
the evident conclusion that the lure of real or fancied advantages in the New World did just as much as the disadvantages of

the Old to induce the Highlanders to leave Scotland. As early as
the eighteenth century those who had served abroad in the
British armies brought back stories of North America. Obviously
such descriptions could conjure up the most hopeful of visions—
visions which colonizers, disinterested or otherwise, were quick
to foster. Eye-witness accounts could be very enticing. In 1787
Samuel Holland, who prepared a complete survey of Cape
Breton, wrote of the island with an enthusiasm surprising in one
who had scrutinized its contours through the precise eye-piece of
a theodolite:

> Nature has blessed few countries with so many advantages as
> this island; for the conveniency and number of its ports, the general
> fertility of the soil, the quantity of timber, the many rivers, rivulets,
> creeks, lakes, coasts, etc., abounding with fish, the innumerable
> game resorting here at different seasons of the year are such induce-
> ments as with a little encouragement would invite many to become
> settlers—especially when it is considered that in raising of corn,
> vegetables, hemp, and flax, in lumber, in potash, but above all in the
> fishery there are such inexhaustible kinds to reward the industry of
> the pursuer, . . . the most avaricious would be satisfied and the most
> diffident emboldened.[15]

Other commentators more likely to reach a Highland audience described the possibilities of Canada in the Gaelic periodicals[16] edited by the Reverend Norman MacLeod of St.
Columba's (Glasgow)[17] between the years 1829 and 1843, and in
hand-books such as Rob MacDougall's *Ceann-Iuil an Fhir-
Imrich do dh' America mu Thuath* (Guide for the Emigrant to
North America), published in 1841.[18] The emigrant's head must
have been filled with a strange mixture of fact and fancy.
Landlords sometimes employed eloquent agents to persuade
unwanted tenants to emigrate, and shipping companies found it
very profitable to send a smooth-tongued salesman among the
Highlanders to gather up human cargo. One of the more notorious of these agents, Archibald McNiven of Islay, claimed to
have transported between the years 1821 and 1832 twelve
thousand Highlanders to Cape Breton, the mainland of Nova
Scotia, Prince Edward Island, and Upper Canada.[19] The
picture of the New World drawn by these subtle propagandists
was often far beyond the bounds of truth. The Bard MacLean,

who settled at Barney's River (Pictou County, Nova Scotia) in 1819, was bitterly disappointed in the land of promise. In his *Oran do dh' America* (Song to America)[20] he complains:

'S i seo an duthaich 's a bheil an cruadal
Gun fhios do'n t-sluagh a tha tigh'nn a nall.
Gur h-olc a fhuaras oirnn luchd a' bhuairidh
A rinn le'n tuairisgeul ar toirt ann.

Bidh gealladh laidir 'g a thoirt an trath sin;
Bidh cliu an aite 'g a chur am meud;
Bidh iad ag raitinn gu bheil ur cairdean
Gu sona saibhir gun dad a dh' eis;
Gach naigheachd mheallta 'g a toirt 'g ur n-ionnsaidh-se,
Feuch an sanntaich sibh dol 'n an deigh;
Ma thig sibh sabhailt nuair chi sibh iadsan
Chan fhearr na statachan na sibh fein.

Nuair theid na drobhairean sin 'g ur n-iarraidh,
'S ann leis na briagan a ni iad feum,
Gun fhacal firinn a bhith 'g a innse
'S an cridhe diteadh na their am beul;
Ri cur am fiachaibh gu bheil 's an tir seo
Gach ni a's priseile tha fo'n ghrein.
Nuair thig sibh innte gur beag a chi sibh
Ach coille dhireach toirt dhibh an speur.

This is the country where there is hardship though the people coming across don't know it. It was evil they brought on us, those enticers, who contrived through their fairy-tales to bring us out here.

Great promises are made at the time; the magnificence of this spot is glorified. They tell you that your friends are happy and prosperous and without lack; by every deceptive report brought to you they try to make you yearn to go across after the others. But if you do get here safely, when you actually see them, their condition is no better at all than your own.

When these cattle-drovers come after you, they do their job with lies, not uttering a word of truth, their heart denying what their mouth says, representing that everything desirable under the sun is in this land. But when you reach it, there's little you'll see but tall forests shutting out the sky from you.

He pleads with everyone who may hear his song to listen to reason,

'S na tugaibh eisdeachd do luchd a' bhosd,
Na faidhean breige a bhios 'g ur teumadh,
Gun aca speis dhibh ach deigh ur n-oir.

and don't give any hearing to the exaggerators, those prophets of
lies who're tempting you without any regard at all for yourselves but
only for your money.

It was well for the emigrants that they were possessed of hope,
even if delusive, for they had a long and perilous road ahead of
them. They were counted lucky when their sailing ship made the
Atlantic crossing within thirty days, and then they could very
well thank Providence that they had not been shipwrecked or
sunk. On the voyage they were exposed to typhus, cholera,
smallpox, dysentery, measles, and starvation.[21] Of the two
hundred passengers carried from Leith and Stornoway in the
summer of 1827 by the *Harmony*, thirteen died during the
crossing, twenty-two died after being put off on some unin-
habited spot of Cape Breton, and five more were dead when the
vessel reached Sydney—a 20 per cent mortality.[22]

Even if emigrants did land safely, their trials were not over:
they had, in many cases, to travel far before they reached the
spot where they intended to settle; they had few friends to
guide them in the new land; and almost invariably they had
very little money. Only occasionally do the records mention
a Highland settler in possession of a sum adequate to his needs.
In 1821, for instance, Hugh Ban Gillis brought out enough
money, realized from the selling of his stock in Barra, to buy a
farm at Christmas Island, which had already been settled and
worked for fifteen years by an earlier Highland settler, who died
just at the time Hugh arrived in Cape Breton.[23] But he was
exceptionally fortunate, for the majority of the settlers possessed
little more than the price of their fare to cross the ocean. It
was this sum, in fact, that often decided their fate.[24] Many
small tenants of the Highlands and Islands still poorer, when
forced to leave their little farms, could not afford to pay the
necessary passage-money. Their only alternative was to move
south and try their luck at making a living in the Lowlands.

Even wealth was not always a reliable helpmate to those
crossing the ocean. The records tell of one Scot—whether
Highland or Lowland is not specified—who set out in 1828 with
property amounting to £500; but he was shipwrecked off
Newfoundland. Although he and his family were rescued, all his

property was lost, and he was left without a penny to support himself and his thirteen children.[25]

Hazardous as the journey was, the Highlanders were not daunted. Even the aged ventured to spend their few remaining years in a new home. Occasionally a census has been preserved which suggests remarkable facts. In a list of newly arrived Highland settlers, prepared in 1815 for the district of Pictou,[26] we find the following:

> Catherine McKay, aged sixty-five;
> Marion McLean, aged seventy;
> John Ross, aged seventy;
> Hugh McIntosh, aged seventy;
> Catherine McKay, aged seventy;
> Angus Murray, aged seventy-two.

Sailing lists reveal the same story. Among the 208 passengers on the *Saint Lawrence* who sailed in 1828 from Greenock in Scotland to Ship's Harbour (Port Hawkesbury), Cape Breton, were the following:

> John MacQuarrie, aged sixty-five;
> Donald MacKay, aged sixty-five;
> Peggy MacLean, aged eighty;
> Rory MacIsaac, aged eighty-five;
> Marion MacMillan, aged eighty-eight;
> Allan MacLean, aged eighty-nine.[27]

Mothers brought with them babes in arms. Children were born during the passage. The *Economy* sailed from Tobermory in 1819 with 285 emigrants. During the leisurely five-week voyage to Pictou four children were born aboard her.[28]

Emigration has, of course, always been a hazardous venture, and parting from the old home must have been equally trying for *Mayflower* Pilgrim or Russian Doukhobor, for Virginian colonist or Italian labourer alike. In the continuity of human experience the Highlanders too felt the tug of separation. Mrs. Matheson, comfortably settled in Little Narrows, Cape Breton, can vouch for that; she well remembers her father, who came from the island of Lewis as a young lad, telling his children, "If there's any place in the world I'd like to visit, it's back to see the island of Lewis again." Mrs. MacAskill of Englishtown, Cape

Breton, recollects that her father wasn't happy to leave his native island either. He was planning to build a new house there, but when he assembled the stone, the landlord heard of his intentions and wouldn't allow him to continue. Though he came to Cape Breton, he too would always speak of Lewis as the finest place in the world.

Gaelic songs composed by the immigrants reflect the same nostalgia.

> 'S e tigh'nn a thamh do'n ait' s' as ur
> A dh' fhag mo shuilean dall.
> Nuair sheol mi 'n iar, a' triall bho m' thir,
> A Righ, gur mi bha 'n call.
>
> Dh' fhag mi 'n duthaich, dh' fhag mi 'n duthchas;
> Dh' fhan mo shugradh thall,
> Dh' fhag mi 'n t-aite baigheil, caomh,
> 'S mo chairdean gaolach ann.
> Dh' fhag mi 'n tlachd 's an t-ait' am faict' e,
> Tir nam bac 's nan carn.
> 'S e fath mo smaointinn bho nach d' fhaod mi
> Fuireach daonnan ann.

Coming for the first time to stay in this place has blinded my eyes with tears. When I sailed off west, leaving my land, O Lord, it's then that I suffered a loss!

I left my country, I left my heritage. My spirits remained behind. I left that warm and friendly place and my dear friends there. I left my affection in the place to which it was attached—the land of banks and braes. The cause of my brooding is that I wasn't allowed to stay there forever.

This is a part of the song [29] that John the Hunter MacDonald composed after leaving Lochaber in 1834 and settling in Mabou, Cape Breton. His heart-cry may be taken as typical of the feelings that troubled many a dispirited Highlander before he had hacked out a new home for himself amid the stubborn spruce.

It could have afforded no consolation to the exile to reflect that his countrymen in Scotland—many of them deserted by the most enterprising of their sons and daughters—were lamenting the separation just as much as he. The Reverend Norman MacLeod of St. Columba's, who witnessed many melancholy

farewells, wrote a sketch entitled *Long Mhor nan Eilthireach*
(The Emigrant Ship)[30] which, even if now somewhat dated in its
sentimentalism, convincingly recaptures the grief of those who
were left behind. A blind and aged man calls out to his daughter,
who is departing with her family:

> "Dh' fhalbh sibh! Dh' fhalbh sibh! Dh' fhagadh mise 'm aonar
> an diugh gu dall aosda, gun bhra-thair, gun mhac, gun chultaice;
> agus an diugh—la mo dhunach, Dia 'thoirt maitheanais domh—tha
> thusa, Mhairi, mo nighean, m' aon duine cloinne, le m' oghachan
> geala, gaolach, a' dol 'gam fhagail.
>
> "Tillidh mis' an nochd do'n ghleann ud thall; ach chan aithnich
> mi an lamh a tha 'gam threorachadh. Cha tig sibhse, a leanaban mo
> ghraidh, a mach an coinneamh an t-seann-duine; cha chluinn mi
> tuilleadh briagail ur beoil ri taobh na h-aibhne; . . . nuair a chluinn-
> eas mi tathunn nan con, cha leum mo chridhe na's fhaide, 's chan
> abair mi, 'Tha mo leanaban a' teachd.' "

> "You have gone, gone! Today I have been left behind lone, blind,
> and aged, with neither brother, nor son, nor supporter; and today—
> the day of my ruination, God forgive me—you, Mary, my daughter,
> the only one of my children, you are going to leave me, you, and my
> dear, lovely grandchildren.
>
> "Tonight I'll go back over to the glen; but I'll not recognize the
> hand that is guiding me. You won't come out, my beloved children,
> to meet the old man. No longer am I going to hear the babble of your
> voices by the river's side. . . . No longer will my heart jump up
> when I hear the dogs barking; never again shall I say, 'My children
> are coming.' "

Whether the depopulation of the Highlands also affected the
feelings of the now powerless hereditary chieftains is hard to
divine. Despite the allegations of the *Boat Song*, it seems
improbable that each and every one of them was a degenerate
lord, content to boast his sheep. But as he watched the ships
carrying his kinsmen overseas, whatever his attitude, every
chieftain must have been compelled to recognize that the
ancient organization of the clan was now forever broken.

3

Settling the New Home

As WE PASS with the adventurers from the Old World to the New, we lose sight of their grief and suffering; we are aware only of their hopes and their opportunities. They did not all settle in easy places. The climate of North Carolina was pleasanter than anything they knew in Scotland; Glengarry County in Ontario was not unduly severe; but Prince Edward Island and the eastern section of the Nova Scotia mainland and the island of Cape Breton faced the settlers with two extremes of climate unknown to them in Scotland: deep snow and bitter cold in the winter and burning heat in the summer. In retrospect we may easily feel that they had small cause for thanksgiving. Rough, untamed forest-land was all that a place such as Cape Breton might seem to offer, yet their wondering eyes saw possibilities in it, and their attack on the problems of settling won admiration from those who saw them at work.

When the Imperial government in 1827 suggested ridding England of unwanted paupers by sending them to Cape Breton, assisted by government allowances, the Surveyor-General of Cape Breton vehemently rejected the scheme, saying that "the lazy inmates of poor-houses . . . would sink into despair at the sight of our stubborn forests and terrific winters."[1] He contended that "the people who had of late years settled among us . . . were much better suited to this climate and soil than any that the Parent State was desirous of removing."[2] And Dr. Gesner, a geologist who had explored the length and breadth of Nova Scotia and New Brunswick, wrote in 1843:

> Perhaps there are no race of people better adapted to the climate of North America than that of the Highlands of Scotland. The habits, employments, and customs of the Highlander seem to fit him for the American forest, which he penetrates without feeling the

24

gloom and melancholy experienced by those who have been brought up in towns and amidst the fertile fields of highly cultivated districts.

Scotch emigrants are hardy, industrious, and cheerful, and experience has fully proved that no people meet the first difficulties of settling wild lands with greater patience and fortitude.[3]

After the hazardous sea-crossing and journey to their chosen portion of the promised land, the Highlanders were to meet their real trial—that slow, uncertain struggle with nature and the land, the struggle which their descendants still maintain today. But the issue on which they gambled was not, as now, a mere matter of financial profit or loss, but a mortal question of survival or starvation.

How the settlers decided which portion of land to head for in the tree-covered wastes will always remain somewhat of a mystery. Some of them, to be sure, had heard descriptions of their destination. One group of immigrants, for instance, knew just where to aim in the waters of the Bras d'Or Lakes in order to find fertile and convenient farm-sites. First-hand information had been provided them by three soldiers from the island of Barra, Donald Og MacNeil, Donald MacNeil, and Finlay Glas MacKenzie, who had served in the British army on the occasion of the capture of Louisbourg from the French in 1758. During the campaign they had sailed through the Bras d'Or Lakes and had been particularly impressed by the beauty and potentiality of a certain area where the land sloped gently upwards on both sides of a narrow channel. The description they brought back after the wars to Barra was apparently both enthusiastic and precise, for some years later a group of their fellow islanders emigrated to Cape Breton, sailed up the lakes to the very spot, and settled there.[4] The channel is still known in Gaelic as *Caolas nam Barrach* (the Barra Men's Strait), and the settlements on either side of it, now called Grand Narrows and Iona, are peopled by descendants from the kinsmen and friends of the three soldiers.

Other immigrants were not so fortunate. Neill Ruadh Mac-Vicar arrived at Sydney, Cape Breton, from North Uist in the summer of 1831 with his family, and chose to remain in the town for a little time so that he could select a site for his new home at leisure. He put up at a boarding house celebrated for its good fare; but the landlady, a certain Mrs. Ahearn, was famed not merely for good fare but also for high prices. Neil Ruadh soon discovered her rapacity and decided that the other people of the town were little better. In true Highland fashion he voiced his dissatisfaction in a Gaelic song.[5] The first verse he directed against the landlady:

> Mo mhallachd-sa gu siorruidh air cailleach 'Hern;
> Siud far 'm bheil a' bhiasd ann am meadhon baile!
> Theab gu'n d' thug i dhiomsa mo chuid us m' anam
> Air son greim dhe'n bhiadh agus aite 'm fanainn.

My everlasting curse on the old Ahearn woman. That's where the beast is, right in the middle of the town! She practically took my soul and portion from me in exchange for a bite to eat and a place to stay.

The undesirability of Sydney evidently hastened his decision as to where he would settle, for he tells us in the course of his song:

> Tha mi dol am bliadhna do Chataloan,
> Far am bheil na Criosduidhean a muigh romham.
> Fagaidh mi na biasdan ud os mo dheighidh—
> Daoine mora, fiadhaich, us Dia 'n an aghaidh!

I'm going to Catalone this year where Christian people have gone out ahead of me. I'm leaving these beasts here behind me—great, savage people, and ungodly!

Neil's remark that he intends to settle among the Christians in Catalone incidentally provides another clue to the pattern of the various Highland settlements. Naturally enough, when people so clannish as the Highlanders arrived in a strange country, they preferred if possible to settle among pioneers who had come from their particular district in Scotland, who spoke their dialect, and who shared the same religious faith. Neil Ruadh was following the instinct of his fellow countrymen when he chose Catalone as a home, for there he would find other families from North Uist, all Presbyterian. If he had been a MacDonald from South Uist, rather than a MacVicar from North Uist, he would undoubtedly have gone to the Grand Mira district where the Catholics from South Uist had settled.

The settlers' first problem was food. Those who chose, or whom necessity forced, to settle in inaccessible and isolated spots sometimes broke the ground for their new home, planted, and harvested during their first spring, summer, and autumn in the New World, and then took refuge from the bitterness of winter in the home of some generous relation already settled. The first settlers of Grand Narrows, for instance, sailed there from the Gulf shore of the Nova Scotia mainland in the spring of 1803 but returned to their base of operations that winter to stay with relatives.[6] The majority of the immigrants, however, particularly the earliest arrivals, could hardly have been so fortunate.

Occasionally a settler found it necessary to move away from his first site and find a better one. We can imagine, when he decided to abandon his first homestead, how he must have grudged the wasted labour which it had cost him. But the problem of survival drove all vain regrets from his mind. The career of Roderick Hunter MacDonald is noteworthy in this respect.[7] On first coming from Scotland he settled at Boulardrie, Cape Breton, but finding the rights to the land there uncertain, he decided to join his relatives on Prince Edward Island. Being self-reliant and an intrepid seaman, he began building a boat suitable for the journey. He had just finished constructing the boat and was heating tar to caulk the seams when his log-house caught fire and burnt to the ground. Undaunted, he worked so much the faster. He sailed with his family and possessions to Souris on Prince Edward Island without mishap but was disappointed in the prospects for settling there, and in a short time sailed back to Sydney, Cape Breton. From there he made his way to Blackett's Lake, where he finally found a satisfactory farm-site. Here he stayed for the remainder of his life.

The most arduous task facing the Highland settlers, who came in many cases from treeless islands or bare stretches of land on the mainland of western Scotland, was to cut down the dense growth of trees covering every inch of their new land. A song[8] written about 1770 (and reputed to be the first Gaelic song composed in North America) mentions the forests with horror, although the author, John MacRae, had settled in the comparatively benign country of North Carolina:

Tha sinne 'n ar n-Innseannaich cinnteach gu leoir;
Fo dhubhar nan craobh cha bhidh aon againn beo,
Madaidh-allaidh us beisdean ag eibheach 's gach froig.
Gu'm bheil sinne 'n ar n-eiginn bho'n threig sinn Righ Deors'.

> We've turned into Indians right enough; in the gloom of the forest
> none of us will be left alive, with wolves and beasts howling in every
> cranny. We're ruined since we left King George.

The Bard MacLean, who settled in Nova Scotia, where the
irrepressible spruce tree still mocks the farmer's labour, is
much more emphatic in his hatred of the forest; his principal
complaint against the settler's life is directed against the back-
breaking, exhausting job of clearing trees from the land:

> Chan ioghnadh dhomhsa ged 'tha mi bronach,
> 'S ann tha mo chomhnuidh air cul nam beann
> Am meadhon fasaich air Abhainn Bharnaidh
> Gun dad a's fearr na buntata lom.
> Mu'n dean mi aiteach 's mu'n tog mi barr ann
> 'S a' choille ghabhaidh 'chur as a bonn
> Le neart mo ghairdein, gu'm bi mi saraichte
> Us treis air failinn mu'm fas a' chlann.[9]

> It's no wonder that I'm gloomy living here back of the mountains
> in the middle of the wilderness at Barney's River with nothing
> better than plain potatoes. Before I make a clearing and raise crops
> and tear the tyrannous forest up from its roots by the strength of
> my arms, I'll be worn out, and almost spent before my children have
> grown up.

There was nothing else for it, however; the Highlander swung
his axe and levelled the trees. The straightest and soundest logs
he used as timber for his dwelling, which was at first only a one-
room cabin. He and his wife slept in the only bed, if they owned
one at all, and sometimes enjoyed the luxury of a screen. The
children found the best places they could on the floor, sleeping
on straw that had been dried beside the fire. The most vital part
of the house was its fireplace, a vast stone structure. Not only
did it provide warmth and light for the household, but by it
all the cooking was done. An iron crane held the pots over the
flames; roasts were dangled on a chain and turned round and
round before the glowing logs; baking was done in iron pots
placed in the hot embers. The unwelcome forest at least provided plenty of fuel, and it was used lavishly. Back-logs, as
large as the fireplace could accommodate, were dragged to the
house and lowered into place; pushed to the back of the hearth,
they served to keep the fire burning steadily all day.

Fields were cleared for cultivation. After the trees were
chopped down, the stumps were left to rot so that they could be

easily removed. The cut timber was piled in great heaps, as the Bard MacLean ruefully remarked,[10] and burned, the ash furnishing excellent fertilizer:

> Gur h-iomadh ceum anns am bi mi 'n deis laimh
> Mu'n dean mi saibhir mo theachd-an-tir;
> Bidh m' obair eigneach mu'n toir mi feum aisd'
> 'S mu'n dean mi reiteach air son a' chroinn:
> Cur sgonn nan teintean air muin a cheile
> Gu'n d' lasaich feithean a bha 'nam dhruim,
> 'S a h-uile ball diom cho dubh a sealltainn,
> Bidh mi 'gam shamhlachadh ris an t-suip.

Many a labour I'll be involved in before I can make my living secure; my work will be exhausting before I get any returns from it and before I make a clearing for the plough. Piling tree-trunks on top of each other in bonfires has strained every muscle in my back, and every part of me is so black that I'm just like soot.

More impatient settlers risked burning patches of timber down as they stood, a dangerous process. When ground was not needed so urgently, every tree in a stand of timber would be notched in the bark with the axe in such a way that the tree would die. Storms could then perform the heavy work that men would normally have to undertake. One good wind storm, once the trees were dead, would flatten them to the ground.[11]

Fortunately for the Highland settler, the newly cleared ground, the *coille dhubh* (black forest) or *coille loisgte* (burnt forest) as they called it, was magnificently fertile. There was no need for ploughing or cultivating; seed thrown on the new soil sprang up in overwhelming luxuriance, responding as if by magic to the need of those whose hands had scattered it. Fortunate it was, because the Highlanders had learned little in Scotland of the more modern methods of agriculture. Their principal instrument was the *cas chrom* (crooked leg), a simple hand plough something like a narrow, elongated spade.[12] With this instrument they planted their first potatoes among the rocks and stumps of their new land; there are many living today who remember using it.

Just as the untouched earth yielded a rich harvest, so the woods provided game in abundance—deer, caribou, moose, partridge, ducks—and the waters teemed with fish—salmon, herring, cod, mackerel, oysters, lobsters. The stories still current concerning the amazing plenitude of fish and game, and the prodigality with which they were consumed, are almost incredible in our present age of strict conservation. In Cape Breton lobsters could be picked up by hand in any cove on the sea-coast. Moose could be trapped by the dozen by simply chasing them into the deep snow, where they could not move rapidly enough to escape the hunters. So much unused moose-meat accumulated on one of the shores at the north of Cape Breton as the result of this butchery that ships would steer well away from the spot to avoid the stench of the rotting carcasses.[13]

In spite of this apparent abundance the new settlers led a difficult life and were often faced with starvation. Their families were large, and the climate uncertain. Blight and destructive frost destroyed the mainstays of the Highlander's diet, grain and potatoes. Early government records of Cape Breton are full of pathetic pleas for relief which present tragic pictures of misery and starvation. Even the relentless Norman McLeod, minister of St. Ann's, who had once sentenced a boy, on suspicion of theft, to have the tip of his ear clipped off,[14] was touched by the suffering of his parishioners when in 1848 the spring came late and the supplies were almost exhausted. Writing on the first of June in that year he says: ". . . the general destitution has made it impossible, even for the most saving, to shut their ears and eyes from the alarming claims and craving of those around them, running continually from door to door, with the ghastly features of death staring in their very faces; and especially since the expected relief from Government, for both food and seed, has been a mere disappointment."[15]

And even when the settlers lived a life of plenty, they had to work continually with the simplest of instruments. The harvest was cut with the sickle (*corran*), threshed with the flail (*suist*), riddled through a skin-sieve (*criathar*), and ground in a stone hand-mill (*brath*). Regular mills were, of course, soon built, but the hand-mill, or quern, remained a cherished possession in many a household. The Highland housewife had in Scotland done her own milling and thus avoided the exorbitant charge levied by the landlord holding the rights over the local mill, and she therefore felt towards her quern a sort of affection that has no exact counterpart in the heart of the modern housewife. Mrs. Donald Red McNeil brought her quern with her all the way from Barra in Scotland to Pictou in Nova Scotia in 1802, and then from there to Grand Narrows in 1804, when she and her husband resettled.[16]

Besides the endless work of feeding the family, there was also the problem of clothing. After the wool was sheared from the sheep, the women of the household had to comb, card, and spin it, then weave or knit it into clothing and bedding. Clothing was sometimes more elegant than the word "home-spun" would lead one to expect; if one may judge from a home-spun jacket made according to the old style of handicraft in 1887 and still preserved in Catalone, Cape Breton,[17] the early settlers could prepare clothes for themselves as handsome as those produced by the best professional methods today. But warmth was for the first arrivals a much more important consideration than style. The Bard MacLean who felt the change of climate acutely, warned any of his countrymen who might be thinking of coming out to America that the winter costume on this side would be of a fashion new to them:

> . . . ge maith an triubhsair cha dean i feum,
> Gun stocain dhubhailt' 's a' mhogais chludaich
> Bhios air a dunadh gu dluth le eill;
> B' e 'm fasan ur dhuinn a cosg le fionntach
> Mar chaidh a rusgadh de'n bhruid an de.
>
> Mur bi mi eolach air son mo chomhdaich
> Gu'm faigh mi reota mo shron 's mo bheul;
> Le gaoth a tuath a bhios neamhail fuaraidh
> Gu'm bi mo chluasan an cunnart geur.[18]

However good your trousers are, they'll do no good without two pairs of stockings and hair-lined moccasins that are tightly laced with thongs. It's the latest fashion with us to wear the hide, hair and all, just as it comes stripped from the beast the day before.

If I'm not careful about my clothing my nose and lips get frozen; my ears are always in serious danger from the north wind, which is bitter and biting.

The hair-lined moccasins to which the bard refers so ruefully were a kind of shoe made by hand from soft leather, particularly that which was taken from the leg and knee of slaughtered cows. Inelegant as they may have seemed to a man of Mac-

Lean's background, they were the ideal foot-wear for deep snow, according to the testimony of those who remember wearing them, as long as the wearer did not object to the rather gamey smell that lingered with them. Those who preferred less odorous foot-wear adopted an invention familiar to them in Scotland, the *mogan*, as it is called in Gaelic. The *mogan* is a sort of knitted slipper strengthened with several thick layers of cloth sewed onto the sole. Comfortable and reliable in deep, dry snow when tied on tightly over warm stockings, it is still used by the settlers' descendants when they have occasion to go to the woods in the winter for their supply of fire-wood.

Not only did the settler make his own foot-wear, but he turned his ingenuity to the manufacture of all his domestic needs. Whether for barn or church, for furniture or for boat, the pioneers cut and shaped all their building material by hand with only the saw, adze, and axe for tools. They developed a steady hand and a true eye, and found no difficulty in such delicate work as making their own shingles with this primitive equipment. They stripped fibre from the wood of the birch-tree and wove it into rope; or for a better grade of rope, when extra strength was required, they collected horse hair. Shortage of ready-made hardware was for them not a hardship but a challenge.

Today the log-houses have rotted and crumbled; in a few cases the foundations are still visible, but usually little more. Here and there an old stone chimney remains, hidden behind the wall-paper of a new house; hand-carved door mouldings are still preserved in rebuilt homes; the settler's hand-made lounge, a sturdy piece of furniture, still stands in the kitchen; but the houses are now frame.

Whatever the trials besetting the pioneer as he cleared, built, and planted, he was consoled by the realization that he was clearing, building, and planting for himself and for his family. He appreciated the luxury of independence after his experiences in his homeland, and he gloried in the possession of land of his own. He was no longer willing to remain a tenant, as the history of Glenaladale's colonists in Prince Edward Island clearly proves. The laird had purchased a large tract of land and brought out his 250 retainers to the island at his own expense, but, when he offered them individual subsections within his property at a reasonable rent, with a lease for 990 years, he found that most of them disliked the idea of continuing to live under the power of a landlord in the New World. They could be satisfied only by outright possession and unlimited tenure, and consequently some of them moved away from the laird's land to other unsettled portions of the island, while others sailed to Cape Breton.[19]

The violence with which the Highland immigrants disputed property rights astonished their more peaceful neighbours, who could not understand the Highlander's lust for land. Justice Chipmann, reporting in 1828 on the litigation throughout Nova Scotia, remarked that in one section, now included in Antigonish County, "there are more blighted causes than in many other districts. The class of people here living are chiefly Highlanders, . . . warm in their tempers, stern in defending their rights, and obstinate in resenting supposed or real wrongs and injuries; when they get to law they do not easily give back."[20]

Joseph Howe, an astute commentator, wrote in 1830 of his Highland neighbours in Nova Scotia: "A curious feature in the character of the Highland population spread over the eastern parts of the Province is the extravagant desire they cherish to purchase large quantities of land." But, unlike others, he realized that their urge was the natural result of an upbringing in the mother country where the possession of a few hundred acres could, as he said, raise the owner "to the first circle of rank and influence in the kingdom." And he added to his comment the interesting observation that many settlers were spending all their money in the reckless purchase of more and more new acres when they should be using it to cultivate the ground they already possessed. "They will toil night and day, spend as little as possible, and live upon the commonest fare until a sum of money is saved, either sufficient to buy an adjoining tract, or to pay the fees required to get a grant from the Crown."[21]

Only those who know the pioneer's history can appreciate how dearly the Highlander cherished the land for which he had suffered the sorrows of exile, of loneliness, and of toil.

4

The Folk-Culture Transplanted

Norman MacLeod of St. Columba's Church visited an influential leader of church affairs in Edinburgh. The year was 1824. He explained to his friend that the Highlanders in Scotland had only one edition of the Bible in their own tongue, a tiny volume with microscopic print which was quite useless for any except the young and clear-sighted. He recommended that the Church of Scotland should publish a satisfactory quarto volume in print large and clear enough for even the feeble eyes of the aged to read. When at last the worthy minister thought he had made a favourable impression, the listener rose and said, "That is the breakfast bell; just advise your Highland friends to get spectacles."[1]

"Advise your Highland friends to get spectacles." Incongruous words on the lips of a churchman, they epitomize the indifference of the English-speaking section of Great Britain towards a racial minority set apart by tongue and culture. It was only a little more than twenty years before Norman MacLeod's conversation that any translation at all of the entire Bible into Scottish Gaelic had been circulated among the Highlanders.[2] To be sure, as early as 1686 two hundred copies of the Bible translated into Irish Gaelic had been sent to the Protestant ministers in the Highlands of Scotland for the good of their parishioners; and in 1767 the New Testament had been translated into Scottish Gaelic;[3] but a complete translation was actually opposed by some members of the Society for Propagating Christian Knowledge on the grounds that it would tend to preserve the distinction between Highlander and Lowlander.[4] There were, of course, members of the English-speaking population who were not so bigoted. Samuel Johnson, for one, hurled a characteristic thunder-bolt in support of the Highlanders' cause:

> I did not expect to hear that it could be, in an assembly convened for the propagation of Christian knowledge, a question whether any nation uninstructed in religion should receive instruction; or whether that instruction should be imparted to them by a translation of the holy books into their own language. . . . To omit for a year, or for a day, the most efficacious method of advancing Christianity, in compliance with any purposes that terminate on this side of the grave, is a crime of which I know not that the world had yet an example, except in the practice of the planters of America, a race of mortals whom, I suppose, no other man wishes to resemble.
>
> . . . the efficacy of ignorance has long been tried, and has not produced the consequences expected. Let knowledge, therefore, take its turn: and let the patrons of privation stand a while aside, and admit the operation of positive principles.[5]

But to change public opinion would have required more than the eloquence of Samuel Johnson, who himself underestimated the culture of the Highlanders whom he had on this occasion befriended.[6] English-speaking people have consistently despised Gaelic culture and attempted to eradicate the language. In 1616 an act was passed in Scotland calling for the establishment of parish schools throughout the Highlands in order that English should be implanted among the people, and Gaelic "abolished and removed."[7] In 1701 when the Society for the Propagation of Christian Knowledge established charity schools, the teachers were instructed to discourage scholars from speaking Gaelic.[8] In 1811 the Gaelic Schools Society attempted to remedy the situation by supporting the teaching of Gaelic in some Highland communities, but after thirty-two years of beneficial work the Society collapsed from lack of funds.[9] Even in Nova Scotia, if settlers' children persisted in speaking their mother tongue at school instead of the unfamiliar English, they were either scolded by the gentle teachers or beaten by the impatient. Despite all impediments, however, the language has persisted wherever Highlanders are born or have settled; and now national educational leaders in Scotland, recognizing the mistakes of the past, encourage the teaching of Gaelic.

As for the contempt directed against Gaelic culture, historians have succeeded in dispelling the notion that Highland civilization consists of a mixture of haggis, whisky, bagpipes, and illiteracy. Since haggis and whisky belong to the Lowlands as much as to the Highlands, and bagpipes of various kinds have been used in various parts of the Western world for centuries,[10] these items require no further comment; but the relation of illiteracy to Gaelic culture must be examined more fully.

Scotland once knew a flourishing Gaelic civilization. In the sixth century on the island of Iona in the remote Hebrides, St. Columba initiated missionary and educational enterprises for which the area subsequently became widely renowned.[11] Architects, sculptors, metal-workers, jewellers, weavers, musicians, and poets sprang from the Gaelic colonists who gradually spread over Scotland.[12]

When Queen Margaret began to Anglicize Scotland in the eleventh century,[13] however, Gaelic culture was uprooted in the Lowlands. Losing political control, the Gaelic people were unable to develop a unified system of education which would guarantee literacy in their own language; and tangible evidences of their literary activity are consequently exceptional. In the sixteenth century, for instance, the Lord of the Isles' hereditary physician was capable of compiling in Gaelic a medical handbook remarkable for its enlightened interest in preventive medicine;[14] and we know that the formal study of bardic poetry survived into the eighteenth century, since a technical treatise dealing with bardic prosody is preserved in a Clanranald manuscript of that period.[15] But, in general, as a result of the lack of opportunities for education in the Highlands, many immigrants to the New World could not read or write their mother tongue and could neither speak, read, nor write the English language.

One of the first Presbyterian missionaries to travel among the Highland settlers of Cape Breton[16] estimated in the eighteen-thirties that not more than one-fifth of the heads of families could read, although he noticed that most of those who were young enough to have attended the Gaelic Schools in Scotland before they emigrated were at least literate in their own language. But in the earlier part of the nineteenth century few books had been published in Gaelic, Highland music was almost entirely unrecorded, and the uninformed outside world suspected the Highlanders of being little better than savages. The well-schooled Loyalists in the Maritimes probably felt immensely superior when they watched the bewildered Gaelic-speaking immigrants file down the gang-planks onto the Canadian shore.

Despite, or perhaps because of, their lack of literacy, the Highlanders nevertheless perpetuated a complete culture orally. They brought with them, unseen, a rich heritage of household arts, games, dances, music, and unwritten literature. A favourite proverb runs:

> Thig crioch air an t-saoghal,
> Ach mairidh ceol agus gaol.

An end will come to the world, but music and love will endure.

Most peoples pay fitting respect to love, but if disparagers had realized that the Highlander esteemed music on an equal plane, they would have come much closer to understanding his real nature.

Much of the unrecorded folk-culture brought by the immigrants to the New World can no longer be recovered, but their descendants can even now recollect examples sufficient to suggest its scope.

Gaelic folk-literature, and especially the folk-song, was allied with every activity. Many of the songs were centuries old; scarcely any of them had been written down, but as everyone knew them by heart, that was no matter. For instance, during the fishing season, if there was no wind to fill their sails, the Cape Breton settlers might have to row six or eight miles to tend their nets and lines. It was back-breaking work pulling on sixteen-foot oars on a hot, windless summer day; two men driving a heavy boat against current and tide. But the boatmen knew how to lighten their labour. As they rowed they sang an *iorram*, a boat-song, the tune and measure of which harmonized with the motion of rowing. When a girl went milking (no self-respecting Highland man would, until recently, be seen milking), she also sang the appropriate occupational songs. In fact, tradition claims that some rather pampered cows would not give milk unless she did so.[17]

The housewife too had her stock of folk-poetry to draw from. If she were churning the butter, she would sing playfully as she plunged the dasher up and down in the churn:

> Tha cluig a' seo,
> Tha clag a' seo,
> Tha siliseag mhor bhog a' seo.
> Thig na saoir,
> Thig na maoir,
> Thig fear a' churrac bhuidhe.
> Thig 'n a shruth an t-im.[18]

There's a click here, there's a clack here, there's a great wet mass here. The carpenters will come, the constables will come, the man with the yellow cap will come. The butter 'll come in a rush.

If the baby began to cry, she crooned:

> Ba, ba, mo ghaol.
> Fan tosdach, samhach.
> Ainglean naoimh'
> Gu'n dean do shuan.
> Beannachdan
> Ro mhor, gun aireamh,
> Thigeadh ort
> Gach la 'nuas.[19]

Hush, hush, my dear. Stay still and quiet. Holy angels grant you sleep. May blessings many, without number, come down upon you every day.

And so it was with every other activity. Old rimes and songs welled up from the depths of memory.

No event made greater demand on the repertoire of folk-songs than the milling frolic, when the home-woven blankets were waulked or fulled—that is, worked until a nap was raised on the surface of the home-spun yarn. Highland women had never resorted to the fulling mill generally used for this purpose; they did the work by hand, or sometimes by foot, and in the process they always found occasion for song and amusement. When a housewife had accumulated her winter's weaving, the young men and girls gathered in her home. In Scotland the actual work was, and indeed still is, performed by women only. The New World settlers at first continued to exempt the menfolk from such labour, but fifty years ago or more (according to various Cape Breton informants) the women became so emancipated that they expected the men to share not merely the pleasure but also the work.

The milling frolic is ingeniously utilitarian. The participants perform a necessary task, but they convert the occasion into a source of entertainment for the community. It is therefore not surprising that, of all the Highland customs still surviving in the New World, it is the most honoured and best preserved. Anyone who wishes to recapture a taste of the settlers' life in Cape Breton may, by joining in a milling frolic, still witness a scene not very different from what he might have viewed a hundred years ago. A specially grooved board or sturdy planks are secured to heavy trestles to form a solid work-table. The workers sit at either side of it, about six or seven on each side. Two half-widths of blanket are sewn endlong to form a continuous band, then moistened and soaped and presented to the company to mill. The workers pound the cloth down on the boards with a slightly lateral rubbing motion designed to raise a nap and then swiftly flick it up to the left away from the hands of one person and into the hands of the next. Rhythmically they beat the cloth until the boards fairly hum. The very floor of the house seems to rise and fall under the heavy cadence, and the cloth moves so fast that it becomes a wild, whirling circle abruptly soaring and dropping.

To lighten this heavy work a strong-voiced singer leads off a milling song (*oran luaidh*), the beat of which is perfectly adapted for the rhythm of the work. After each stanza everyone joins in the chorus. The song lasts for perhaps ten or twelve stanzas, concluded usually by a burst of laughter. The pound and flick are still maintained. The leader starts off another song. And so the evening continues. New hands slip into the places at the table deserted by the first comers, who soon tire despite the fact that the labour is lightened by music. Those who are not taking part fill in the time by joining in the singing, by conversation, and by dancing.

Before they emigrated from Scotland, the Highlanders in some areas had been instructed by severe spiritual advisers that singing was sinful. But even those who accepted this gloomy advice were inclined to be tolerant on the occasion of a milling frolic. An elderly woman living on the shores of St. Ann's Bay in Cape Breton recollects, with amusement tempered by the respect she feels for the past, that in her home the assembled guests would wait for the consent of her grandfather before they started to sing. Her grandfather was a MacLeod from Lewis and evidently belonged to the strict set. But even he would grudgingly admit, "If there's any good at all in singing, it's milling and putting the baby to sleep."

After the cloth was satisfactorily fulled—and that might not be until five or six o'clock in the morning—it was carefully wound onto forms to set. This process also called for a song, a "putting up" song, of different metre from the milling song. In keeping with the late hour and the high spirits of the guests, the tone was inclined to be playful. The more knowing matrons would pair off the various girls present with the men who were destined to be their husbands. There were many forms of this "pairing" song and many ingenious impromptu modifications of each form.

One such song consisted of three lines, of which the first and the last were meaningless refrains; the middle line carried the discussion back and forth between the leader of the singing, the other singers, and the individual young man or woman singled out for attention.[20]

The leader would start the process by asking:

> Fal il e lug 's o bo e lug.
> Co an te og a tha seo gun cheile?
> Fal il e lug 's o bo hau.

Fal il e lug 's o bo e lug. What young girl is here without a husband?
Fal il e lug 's o bo hau.

Another singer, casting the answer in the same metrical form and using the same refrain, would pick out the first girl for consideration: "Gur e Mairi tha gun cheile." (It's Mary that has no husband.) The leader would pick up the song again and ask Mary: "Co fear og a gheibh mi fhein dhuit?" (What young man shall I choose for you?) The young girl might cautiously reply: "Nach toir thu mo leannan fhein dhomh?" (Won't you give me my sweetheart?) The leader would then suggest some boy by name: "Gur e Calum bheir mi fhein dhuit." (It's Malcolm that I'll give you.)

But perhaps Malcolm might not suit Mary's fancy. She would mockingly reject him as too inactive: "Luideanach odhar a theid fodha, nach eirich." (A dirty sloven who'd fall down and not rise.) Another might be suggested for her, and she might object against him that he was not able-bodied enough: "Maide air an abhainn, cha tomhais e leum air." (With a stick on the river he couldn't jump over it.) Or she might suggest that some other girl was after him: "Tha te eile 'n toir an deidh air." (There's another girl in pursuit who's in love with him.)

The leader would then be obliged to suggest some more satisfactory companion for the girl: "Gur e Neill a bheir mi fhein dhuit." (It's Neil that I'll give you.) And this time if the name suggested was acceptable, the girl might signify her approval by singing the praises of the boy: "Cridhe glan soluisd am broilleach a leine." (A pure heart of light in the bosom of his shirt.) Or she might offer some less direct reply which still, however, signified approval: "Na'm biodh min agam, bheirinn dha deirce." (If I had meal, I'd give him alms.)

As a final crowning touch to the evening, when the cloth had been milled and put up, it was sometimes, especially in Catholic communities, consecrated by means of an ancient formula. The stately rite is now almost forgotten in the New World, even in Cape Breton where so many Gaelic traditions survive. The details of the custom have been preserved, however, in Alexander Carmichael's collection of Highland lore, which he recorded in Scotland during the nineteenth century.[21] In his account we may still read the dignified formula and recapture the impressive beauty with which the Highlanders, both in the Old World and in the New, invested the simple activities of their daily life. Three consecrators placed the web of cloth on the milling table. Then the eldest revolved it once in a sunwise direction, saying,

> Cuirim an deasalt
> Am freasdal Athar.

I make a sunwise turn in the service of the Father.

The second eldest next went through the same motion, saying:

> Cuirim an deasalt
> Am freasdal Mic.

I make a sunwise turn in the service of the Son.

And the youngest followed, saying:

> Cuirim an deasalt
> Am freasdal Spioraid.

I make a sunwise turn in the service of the Spirit.

Then the three together said:

> Agus gach deasalt
> Am freasdal Teora,
> 'S gach car a theid dha
> An sgath Teora.
> Agus gach deasalt
> Am freasdal Teora.

And each sunwise turn in the service of the Trinity, and each rotation made on it for the sake of the Trinity. And each sunwise turn in the service of the Trinity.

The poetry of the Gael was interwoven even into the medical lore of the settlers. In a country where doctors and veterinaries were almost unobtainable, cures were attempted by home-made medicines. Mare's milk, for instance, was recommended for those suffering from whooping-cough. Herbs were mixed in various ways to allay the most widespread varieties of human suffering. This mystic art is now almost completely forgotten, so that we can no longer reconstruct the details.

In cases where medicine was of no avail, a type of faith-cure was attempted by the use of charms. If a horse had a sprained foot, his owner resorted to the *Eolas an t-Sniomh* (Charm for the Sprain). He would knot a string in a special manner around the horse's damaged leg and recite as he did so:

> Thainig Criosd a mach;
> Fhuair e cnamhan an eich
> Air bristeadh mu seach.
> Chuir e fuil ri fuil
> Agus feoil ri feoil;
> Mar leighis e sin,
> Gu leighis thu seo.[22]

Christ came out; he found the bones of a horse broken apart. He placed blood to blood and flesh to flesh; as he cured that, so cure this.

Such charms would work on humans as well as animals. Tooth-ache could be cured by *Eolas an Deideidh* (Charm for Toothache); sties in the eye could be removed by *Eolas nan Sul* (Charm for the Eyes). In order that the cure might be effective, the proceedings had to be taken seriously, and in most cases there were complicated stipulations to be observed. The Charm for the Eyes had to be recited by three people of the same first name—by three Maries, or three Duncans, for instance.

The efficacy of some cures depended on surprise. In such cases one wonders whether the cure was not perhaps more intolerable than the disease itself. An elderly Highland lady of the Mira district in Cape Breton remembers what happened to a friend suffering from jaundice. While he was innocently chatting in a neighbour's kitchen, the host resolved to attempt a traditional cure; unnoticed he stole up from behind with a pail of ice-cold water and confidently emptied it over the patient's back. Then he gave orders for a dry suit of clothes to be brought to his electrified victim and affably explained that the only sure cure for jaundice was a sudden shock. In time the malady departed, but whether because of Nature's working or the cure we shall never know.

In some very difficult cases of sickness, where no other cure was known, many Highland settlers trusted in the powers of any man who had been born the seventh consecutive son in a family. The seventh son was known to cure an invalid by merely visiting him, and his touch was as efficacious as a king's in expelling scrofula (the King's Evil).

The whims of the weather and the seasons were reduced to rationality through the weather sayings that the settlers brought with them from Scotland. These tended to be more colourful than the usually pallid little rimes that have survived among English-speaking people, such as "Rainbow at morning, sailors take warning. Rainbow at night, sailor's delight." The following dialogue is typical:

> Thuirt an Gearran ris an Fhaoiltheach,
> "C' an dh' fhag thu 'n gamhainn bochd?"
> "Dh' fhag mi e 's a shuil air an t-sop."
> "Ma dh' fhag thusa a shuil air an t-sop,
> Cuiridh mise a sheich air an sparr."

Labhair an sin am mios Mart,
"Ma gheoibh mi aon seideag an annail am barr a chluas,
Cuiridh mi 'earball air a ghuaillean.
Suas an t-Earrach." [23]

To understand this rime, we must first understand that
Faoiltheach is the name given to the last fortnight of winter and
first fortnight of spring; Gearran is the even more difficult
period following this when the feed for cattle runs to its lowest
ebb and the weather is apt to be as yet unfit for grazing:

Said Gearran to Faoiltheach,
"Where did you leave the poor yearling calf?"
"I left him with his eye on the straw."
"If you left his eye on the straw,
I'll put his skin on the beam."
Then the month of March says,
"If I get one puff of my breath over his ears,
I'll put his tail to his shoulders.
Then the Spring will be over."

Faoiltheach has left the calf anxious about his future food
supply; Gearran is going to try to starve him completely, so
that the farmer will have to skin him and leave his hide hanging
to cure in the barn; benign March promises, however, that if
she gets a chance, her wholesome wind will send the animal out
to scamper on the pasture, and blessed summer will arrive.

Colourful as these weather sayings are, it is to be hoped that
the settlers did not put too much faith in their validity for the
climate of the New World. All too often they must have found
that the breath of March didn't set the calves to frisking as it
might have in Scotland, but instead sent a delayed winter snow-
storm two or three feet deep. Many a poor yearling must have
yielded up his hide to the beam. Highland settlers in Cape
Breton tell facetiously of the early days when the cattle were so
weak from undernourishment in the spring that it was necessary
to carry them out of the stable to pasture in a wheelbarrow and
prop up their strengthless legs with staves. But there is a certain
element of truth in the exaggeration, which reminds us how
precarious was the livelihood of the first settlers.

Gaelic folk-culture played an important part in the everyday
activities of the Highlander and a still greater part in his leisure

time. However little of the precious gift of leisure the toiling settler may have enjoyed, the culture of his forefathers provided him with a liberal fund of entertainment. When the dusk of evening crept over the land and the tasks of the day were abandoned, the people gathered at the home of the most talented local entertainer. Their chief delight at such a *ceilidh* (gathering) was to lie in the warmth of the great fire, watch its glowing light play on the walls of the house, and listen to *sgeulachdan*, the ancient folk-tales of the Gael. Although the practised reciters have vanished from the land and the tales themselves can be recollected only by few, the impression they made still remains on the minds of the people who used to listen to them. Some remember the thrill of hearing a skilful story-teller as he worked up his audience with a favourite tale; others remember the terror they felt as they hastened home through the darkness and shadows of night after a particularly weird and unearthly story.

The Highlander, like his Irish cousin, possessed a rich heritage of folk-tales. A portion of his repertoire, enshrining the deeds of ancient legendary figures such as Finn MacCoul, Diarmid, and Greine, belonged exclusively to the Celtic people.[24] But the Gaelic story-teller could draw from an even larger store—that great international stock of tales, apparently common to all peoples, which pass swiftly and silently from country to country. The Highlander in Cape Breton has preserved, for instance, a story known to folklorists as "The Clever Peasant Girl." In synopsis, the version recalled by an informant at Christmas Island runs as follows:

> A poor man touches the fabulously valuable golden plough belonging to the king of the land and must, as a penalty, estimate its value correctly. His sharp-witted daughter instructs him to answer the king that, however valuable it may be, it is not so valuable as a shower of rain in the warm month of July. The king, impressed by the answer, orders the girl to appear before him neither clothed nor naked, neither riding nor walking, and neither in the palace nor outside the palace. She comes before him robed in a herring net; she travels on the back of a pig with her feet touching the ground; she sets the animal's front feet over the threshold and hind feet outside.
>
> Greatly impressed, the king says that, if only she were the daughter of a king or of a landed proprietor, he would like to marry her but that, since she isn't, he would like to give her some reward

for her trouble. She answers that she wishes only to be left alone with her father in peace; but, when the king insists on some request, she asks that her father be granted a certain worthless desert island off the shore. When the king makes over the land to her father, she points out that her father has become a landed proprietor, and the king now feels free to marry the clever peasant girl.

The king makes his new wife understand that if she ever opposes his judgment in matters of law she will be turned out of the palace. She, however, stipulates the right to take with her three armfuls of property if she should ever be ejected for this reason. Soon she has cause to show an understanding of law superior to the king's, and he orders her to leave the palace. Accordingly she first carries out her three armfuls: her child in the cradle, then the royal crown, and finally the king himself in his throne. The king, touched by her affection, forgives her and puts her in charge of his legal affairs, and they live happily ever after.

Any child familiar with the fairy-tales collected by the Grimm brothers will recognize the general plot of this story, versions of which scholars have found in many widely scattered parts of Europe, all the way from Ireland to Lapland and from Portugal to Turkey, and as far east as the Indies and China.[25] The *blasé* urbanite of modern times, far removed from the influences of folklore, knows something of a similar type of amusement, for the perennially popular funny story is a member, however uncouth and undistinguished, of the great family of folk-tales, passing as it does by word of mouth across the country. But the tales of the Highlander belong to a more finished and artistic branch of the family and were eloquently and skilfully narrated.

Since the material of the folk-tale was drawn so extensively from the supernatural, the Protestant clergy in Scotland disapproved strongly of this innocent form of entertainment on the ground that it encouraged superstition among the people. Apparently, however, their attacks did not succeed either in weakening the popularity of the folk-tales or in shaking the Highlander's belief in the stories which he so much enjoyed, for even the wildest of them were still regarded as true by many of the Highland settlers who came to this country during the previous century. As early as 1567 we find a man of religion condemning the Gaels in Scotland for their interest in what he labelled "vain, hurtful, lying, worldly stories."[26] And as late as

1921 we find another man of religion writing of the Highland settlers in Cape Breton: "Perhaps the only bad traits that they brought with them to Cape Breton were their superstitions regarding witches, fairies, ghosts, etc., and their fondness for whisky."[27]

Their acceptance of the supernatural elements in their folk-literature and their trust in the curative effects of forbidden incantations were not the only ground upon which the settlers were accused of being superstitious. They believed in the "second sight" (*an da shealladh*), a power which caused those who possessed it to see uncomfortable visions of events which had not at the time taken place. The person thus endowed might, for instance, see a phantom funeral party passing down the road escorting the remains of a man who was then still robust and little expecting to die, but who actually died soon afterwards. Even those who were not normally endowed with this power might occasionally see a "forerunner" (*taibhs*) of something that would later come to pass—perhaps the spectre of a railroad engine thundering through the forest, the glare of its bright headlight lighting up the darkness of the night, at a time when no railroads had been constructed in the country but at a place where a railroad was later laid out. Many of the settlers dreaded the power of "the evil eye" which might be exerted in numerous sinister ways. Thus the Witch of Mull River, for example, was able to transfer the milk from her neighbours' cows to her own, and when she went begging among the pioneering Highlanders in the district (in Cape Breton) none of them dared to refuse her for fear that she might use the power of her evil eye for some more dreadful purpose.[28]

But modern scepticism in sweeping away these manifestations of the imagination has dealt perhaps too harshly with the folk-tale, condemning its art because it relies on a belief in the existence of the *sithichean*, the "little people." Recently a minister in Cape Breton asked the young nephew of a woman who was famed in her day as a reciter of the old Highland stories whether he had inherited a knowledge of any of them. "Och," answered the boy, half contemptuously and half dis-

approvingly, "I don't know any of them. Besides, what's the
use of those stories? Everybody knows now that there aren't any
sithichean any more."

If the *sithichean* have passed away, they deserve a reverent
funeral, for the tales—once so dear to the Highlanders—in
which they figured sharpened the imagination of the pioneers.
The folk-tales provided the illiterate settler with a vivid and
living literature. He required no libraries of fiction to while
away his time. The local story-reciter, or "shennachie" (spelt in
Gaelic *seanachaidh*), could provide him with hours of entertainment, sometimes by reciting only one long story. Gaels in Cape
Breton remember listening to stories that lasted for more than
three hours at a stretch. The minds of those who perpetuated
this folk-culture were richly stocked. And even when a neighbourhood began to grow tired of the repertoire of the local
entertainers, there was always the possibility that a visitor
would come to the district and bring with him a fresh fund of
tales. Young and old would gather at the house where he was
lodging; he would be called on to recite what he knew according
to the traditional formula:

> A' chiad sgeul air fear an taighe,
> Sgeul gu la air an aoidh.[29]

The host owes the first tale; the guest owes tales until day.

Prose narratives were not the only form of folk-literature in
favour at a *ceilidh*. The best-informed entertainers could also
recite long narrative poems[30] similar in content to the folk-
tales dealing with Celtic legend, but perhaps because of the
ornateness and unfamiliarity peculiar to the vocabulary of
these remarkable lays, they have faded from the memory of the
settlers' descendants more completely than the folk-tale. The
less elaborate folk-song has been perennially popular in the
New World. Its vigorous survival may be due in part to its
association with the milling frolic, but songs were likely to be
in demand on many other occasions besides.

Concerning the oral tradition of folk-songs a Gaelic proverb
aptly says:

Is math a dh' fhimireadh an dan a dheanamh, 's a liuthad fear-millidh a tha aige.

A poem would need to be well made, in view of the number of bunglers who'll be at it.

These authorless waifs of Highland music seem to have been well made. The passing years have not diminished their grace, nor have the many bunglers succeeded in defacing them. Though *Fear a' Bhata* (The Boatman)[31] has been often sung, it still retains freshness and poignancy. The deserted girl scanning the sea for her roving lover sings a lament which will have meaning as long as trusting women fall in love with fickle men:

> 'S tric mi foighneachd do luchd nam bata
> Am fac' iad thu, no 'm bheil thu sabhailt;
> Ach 's ann a tha gach aon diubh 'g raitinn
> Gur gorach mise ma thug mi gradh dhuit.
>
> Thug mi gaol dhuit, 's chan fhaod mi aicheadh;
> Cha ghaol bliadhna, 's cha ghaol raidhe,
> Ach gaol a thoisich 'n uair bha mi m' phaisdein,
> 'S nach searg a chaoidh, gus an claoidh am bas mi.

I'm often asking the seamen, did they see you and are you safe; but then each one of them answers that I'm foolish to give my love to you.

I gave my love to you, and I can't deny it. It's not a love of years or seasons, but a love that began when I was just a child, and it'll never wither till death overpowers me.

Songs did not, however, spring only from the secret depths of the folk-memory. In this particular respect the Gael cannot be called illiterate, at least after the year 1841, when John MacKenzie published a celebrated work, *Sar-Obair nam Bard Gaelach* (Masterpieces of the Gaelic Bards).[32] His anthology of Gaelic poetry was enthusiastically received by Highlanders on both sides of the Atlantic. Collections of poetry had appeared previously, but no other volume had such a remarkable effect on the cultural life of the Gaels. Its pages enticed the curious into learning how to read their own language, and those who could already read shared its literary wealth with their neighbours.

Though the volume was a product of machine-culture, the Gaels turned its contents into a folk-possession.

The reverence which the Highlanders felt for their national anthology is illustrated by an anecdote told of one of the later-day bards, William Livingston of Islay (Uilleam MacDhun-leibhe, am Bard Ileach).[33] A young Highland boy arrived in Glasgow and was not sure whether he ought to continue attending the Highland Church in the city or to go to the English-speaking church. He consulted the worthy William, and the bard answered without hesitation:

> Rach thusa do'n Eaglais Ghaidhealaich far an cluinn thu Gaidhlig air a labhairt; leubh do Bhiobull Gaidhlig agus *Sar-Obair nam Bard*; agus chan eil diabhull an Ifrinn a chuireas iteag asad.

> Go to the Highland Church where you'll hear Gaelic spoken; read your Gaelic Bible and *Sar-Obair nam Bard*; and there's not a devil in Hell that'll pluck a pin-feather from you.

No Gael relished this book more than the emigrant Highlander far from his native land. The respect paid to it by the settlers remains among their descendants. Old copies of the first edition may still be found in remote farm-houses in quiet corners of the New World; and two features of this cherished family possession are always apparent: the book has been handled with great care and is still well preserved; and the pages have been read and re-read, turned and re-turned, until they have grown glazed and grey with finger-prints. The demand for *Sar-Obair nam Bard Gaelach* has continued consistently since the first edition was put on sale. In addition to several reprintings in Scotland, a special edition was published in Halifax, Nova Scotia, in 1863 to meet demands in the New World. And even today, now that supplies of the most recent reprint, published in Scotland in 1909, have been exhausted, enthusiastic Gaels search hopefully for second-hand copies.

No doubt some Victorian households of English poetry-lovers wore out the covers of their *Golden Treasury*, but however highly Palgrave's collection may have been esteemed by members of the educated classes it never won its way into the homes of farmer and fisherman and into the heart of the people as did MacKenzie's anthology of the works of the bards.

It would be difficult to enumerate all the occasions on which the Highland settlers cheered their hearts with verse and song. The festivities of New Year were an occasion for poetry. On *Oidhche na Calluinn* (New Year's Eve) it was the custom for the young people to call on their neighbours; and then, more than on any other occasion, the laws of Highland hospitality demanded that the host should treat the guests to the best of his means. But before any caller could be admitted to a house he had to knock at the door and recite a suitable rime, or *duan* as it was called in Gaelic. Sometimes these rimes were long and elaborate, sometimes blunt and playful:

> An gaol an fhortain,
> Leig a stigh bho chuil na comhla sinn;
> Bheir dhuinn deoch de shugh dh' an eorna;
> Tha fios agad fhein gu'n cord e rinn.[34]

For the love of Fortune, let us in from behind the door; give us a drink of barley liquor; you yourself know that we like it well.

Many of the favourite rimes had been imported from Scotland, but some were manufactured, often on the spur of the moment, in the New Land. Some settlers observed *Oidhche na Calluinn* on Christmas Eve rather than New Year's, but their customs and rimes were of the same nature:

> Tha mise 'n nochd a' dol air challaig,
> Innseadh dhoibh gur e maireach Nollaig,
> 'S mur a toir iad domhsa callaig,
> Spionaidh an fheannag an t-suil asta.[35]

I'm going tonight for Christmas Eve treats, telling you that tomorrow is Christmas Day; and if you don't give me a treat, may the crow pluck out your eyes.

As an everyday amusement the settlers were very fond of riddles, and these likewise were cast in verse. The usual riddle describes in highly figurative language an object which the answerer must identify. The anonymous composers would no doubt be amused to know that the settlers' descendants can recall some riddles perfectly but have forgotten the answers; and as anyone knows who has studied poetic riddles such as those in the Old English *Exeter Book*, the solution, once gone, deftly eludes recapture. In most cases, however, the riddle and the answer are preserved intact. The following typical example was brought from the island of Harris to Cape Breton more than a century ago, and the grandson of the settler who brought it can still recite it and provide the solution:

> Chunna mi iongnadh an diugh,
> Mi seoladh air muir:
> Damh gun fhionadh, gun fheoil,
> A' spionadh feoir a talamh dubh.[36]

I saw a wonder today as I sailed on the sea: an ox without hair, without flesh, dragging grass from black earth.

The answer is that the speaker, looking inshore from shipboard, saw a harrow at work, clawing the grass away from the soil with its sharp teeth.

By its peculiar appeal to wonder-loving minds the riddle serves as a genial mentor to children, sharpening their powers of observation and imagination, and developing their command of words. Even this humble member of the literary family played a functional role in the pattern of pioneering life.

Another minor yet honourable literary form still thriving in oral tradition is the proverb, or, to translate the Gaelic term literally, the "old-word." The Highlander respects its inherited wisdom so highly that he says, "Ged a sharaichear an seanfhacal, cha bhreugnaichear e." (Although the old-word may be strained, it will not be belied.) It is useless, however, to quote examples of proverbs from the copious collections in print since the pungency of the "old-word" arises from its reapplication to contexts that are new. The proverb often enhances the comic, and sometimes the pathetic, in conversation; but to illustrate this fact we should have to reproduce the conversation entire.

Second only to his interest in folk-literature was the Highlander's interest in folk-history. In the prosperous days of clan supremacy in Scotland before the collapse of 1746 each chief kept in his household a family historian who was an expert in genealogy and clan history. The pedigree that he could supply for this chieftain might be in part unreliable when designed to support the prestige and claims of the chief,[37] yet the fact remains that the historian carried in his mind with extraordinary retentiveness a mass of details that would put the professional genealogist of today, with his reference books and records, to shame. It was considered no great task to recite the chief's ancestors back for sixteen or twenty generations in the Gaelic manner: Donald son of Lauchlan son of Duncan son of Donald, and so on.

This traditional interest in family ties continued among the Highland settlers in the New World. It is still a matter of pride among their descendants to trace their forbears back to the Highlands and Islands from which they came. Without the aid of any documents many a third and fourth generation descendant in Nova Scotia who visited Scotland during the First or the Second World War was able to trace out his remotest relations. It is not uncommon in Cape Breton to find those who can name their father, grandfather, great-grandfather, all of whom were perhaps born on this side of the Atlantic, and their great-great- and great-great-great- and great-great-great-great-grandfathers, who were born in Scotland. The genealogy flows readily from their lips as they recite their *sloinneadh* (pedigree): "I am Niall mac Lachlainn 'ic Neill 'ic Iain 'ic Lachlainn."[38] "I am Eos mac Neill 'ic Iain 'ic Eachainn 'ic Ghilleasbuig 'ic Fhionnlaigh 'ic Iain."[39] One amateur Highland genealogist, Alexander the Ridge MacDonald, a Gael born in Nova Scotia, was frequently consulted by less well informed Gaels living in Scotland on some of the fine points of their family relationships, and he was able to trace his own paternal line back seven generations to a Highland chief and from him back into the misty past of Gaeldom until his total list included twenty-three names.[40]

The pride shown by the settlers in their ancestry seems all the more remarkable when we realize that only rarely have they derived any material value from their knowledge. There have been cases when a ready knowledge of ancestry has secured a disputed legacy. But as often as not a claim based on oral rather than written information has been swept aside by sceptical lawyers. One man at least living in North America has been defrauded of his rights to the chieftainship of his clan by a claimant in Scotland who, genealogically speaking, had a less sound claim to the honour but had money and a lawyer on his side. Sometimes an irksome legal intricacy has stood in the way of kinsmen who try to claim property bequeathed by their ancestors. The descendants of Jane Innes came from Scotland and settled in

Judique in Cape Breton; here they adopted the name MacInnes.
Jane died and left a large estate to her next of kin. None could
be found in Scotland, but those in Nova Scotia, even though
they could trace the relationship, were no longer eligible for the
legacy since they had changed the form of their name.[41]

But practical or impractical, this genealogical knowledge is an
impressive illustration of what man's memory can retain, un-
trained though it may be by any formal schooling.

The Highland settlers brought with them to America not only
their vast body of folk-literature and history but also a zest for
music. This valued heritage had been severely attacked by the
Protestant clergy, who disapproved of worldly music just as
much as they disliked the "lying stories" so popular among the
Gaels. In Scotland they had succeeded in stamping out the
knowledge and use of the harp and lyre and bellow-pipes; they
had fulminated, although less effectively, against the bagpipes
and the fiddle. Well-meaning, godly elders of the Presbyterian
Church had solemnly smashed the fiddles and burnt the pipes
of those carnally minded people who wished to cling to their
beloved instruments. One of the most pathetic stories among the
minor tragedies of Scotland is told by Alexander Carmichael[42]
about a music-loving native of Eigg who was at last convinced
by the men of God that he should dispose of his violin. Although
it had been made by a pupil of Stradivarius, he allowed himself
to sell it to a pedlar for ten shillings. But his pious renunciation
of worldly music was not deeply rooted, and in his heart he soon
lamented this vile barter:

> Cha b' e idir an rud a fhuaireadh 'n a dail a ghoirtich mo chridhe
> cho cruaidh ach an dealachadh rithe! an dealachadh rithe! agus gu'n
> tug mi fhein a' bho a b' fhearr am buaile m' athar air a son an uair a
> bha mi og.

> It wasn't the thing I got in exchange for it that grieved my heart so
> sorely, but the parting with it! the parting with it! and that I myself
> gave the best cow in my father's fold for it when I was young.

And after he uttered these unhappy words, "the voice of the
old man faltered, and the tear fell. He was never again seen
to smile."

Even in the New World the clergy propagated the bias against
the Highlander's folk-music, but, despite their pious endeavours,

and fortunately for the brighter side of life, the bagpipes and the fiddle were not exterminated, although some settlers' descendants, perplexed by their own conflicting allegiances to religion and to music, still feel a little dubious about them. Illustrations of the part that the bagpipes played in the lives of the pioneers are numerous. When the *Hector* was about to set sail from Scotland in 1773 for Pictou, the captain discovered that a certain John McKay had stolen aboard without paying his fare. The captain was about to set the stowaway ashore again when the Highland passengers discovered what was taking place. John McKay was an able piper; so they pleaded with the captain, offering to share their rations with the extra passenger if he might be allowed to remain on the ship and sail with them to the New World. The captain relented, and the travellers were entertained by the best of bagpipe music while they crossed the ocean.[43] Another band of settlers, who were sailing from Moidart to Prince Edward Island, also enjoyed the good fortune to be accompanied by a piper. A descendant tells that when they landed they formed themselves into sets on the shore and danced a Scotch reel to the music provided by Ronald MacDonald the piper; and Bishop Fraser, who was present at the celebration, exclaimed with delight, "That man has the best little finger on the chanter I have ever known."[44]

Since they could only get a set of pipes from Scotland at great expense, some settlers made their own. Alexander Ban MacIsaac as a young boy was brought in 1843 from Moidart to Giant's Lake in Guysborough County, Nova Scotia. The music which he had heard on the pipes as a child in Scotland echoed in his ear, and he wanted to play it; he owned no pipes, so he contrived a set out of sheepskin and ash-wood and soon became the most popular entertainer in his district.[45] Other Gaels became so proficient in constructing bagpipes that they made a side-line of selling them to musical enthusiasts. Duncan Tailor Gillis, who lived in South-West Margaree, Cape Breton, and later moved to Mira, was so successful at this art that Malcolm Gillis praised him in song:

> 'S mor an onair do na Gaidheil
> A tha tamh an Albainn Nuadh
> Donnchadh Taillear 'bhith 's an tir leo

Cumail ciuil ar sinnsreadh buan.
'S tric a dh' uraich fuaim nam pioban
Caileachd nam fear rioghail suas—
Clann an Gaidheal o na fraochan,
Fir mo ghaoil-sa, laoich nam buadh.[46]

It's a great honour for the Gaels who are living in Nova Scotia that
Duncan Tailor should be with them in this country keeping the
music of our ancestors alive. Often the skirl of the pipes has aroused
the spirits of those kingly men—the Highlanders from the heathery
heath, the people I love, the excellent heroes.

Malcolm might have added that the skirl of the pipes also
played its part in encouraging the Highlanders as they toiled in
the forests of spruce. In enumerating the items necessary for a
new settler, Dr. Gesner remarks: "In a Highland settlement a
set of bagpipes and a player should not be forgotten. I have
known many a low-spirited emigrant to be aroused from his
torpor by the sound of his national music."[47]

Actually the settlers themselves did not require any outside
advice on the matter, for the pipes seem to have become om-
nipresent among them, and for a time remained so among their
descendants. An old-timer from French Road, Cape Breton,
recollects, "When I was young and we went anywhere to visit,
they'd be passing the pipes around from one young man to the
next, and we'd all have to try a tune. Anyone who couldn't
manage that would be so ashamed of himself, he'd try to learn
pretty quick." The pipes were considered suitable, and indeed
almost indispensable, at any occasion, trivial or serious, solemn
or hilarious; the everyday visit, the baptism, the engagement
party, the wedding, the funeral were all graced by the piper's skill.

The fiddle also was produced at any gathering, large or small.
It was especially favoured at moments of quiet relaxation. The
following reminiscence of a music-loving farmer of Highland
descent living in Cape Breton draws a typical picture of the
contribution made by the violin to the amenities of country life:
"Whenever Angus would call on me, he'd ask me to get out my
fiddle. He'd lie down on the floor with his back leaning on a
turned-over chair-back and beat out the time of the music with
his foot while I played. He used to say that there was no more
pleasant way in the world to take a rest. Often he would know a
set of words to sing along with the tune that I was playing. One

of his favourite refrains started out: 'A chaora chrom, c'aite bheil thu?' [O sheep with the crooked horn, where are you?] He'd sing that one over and over for as long as I was willing to play the tune."

To appreciate fully this pleasant vignette of rural contentment we should understand that for the Highlander a reference to the sheep with the crooked horn had a special meaning, and the animal in question was well worth seeking. In the words of the refrain, "all sheep have milk, but this one has a gallon." "The sheep with the crooked horn" is, in fact, the nickname given to the spiral outlet from the Highlanders' home-made (and illicit) whisky-still.[48]

Thus the diverse folk-culture of the Highlander served in many ways to cheer the heart of the settler. Life for him was something more than a ceaseless round of cutting, burning, ploughing, planting, sowing, and reaping; and for his wife, some-thing more than a grim monotony of cooking, carding, spinning, weaving, knitting, sewing, and mending. Their long hours of toil and their few well-deserved moments of leisure were always the occasion for laughter and story and song and music.

The old people who remember something of the bygone way of life are pleased that their children have found easier methods of working and greater opportunities to profit from their labour; yet they never speak of their own experience with regret or resentment. When they recall the old days, they may perhaps say, "Ah, indeed, it was many a roll of cloth I'd be weaving in those days." But they will immediately continue: "Those were the days when you could have fun. If a stranger would come, it wouldn't take long to gather enough people for a dance. There were seven young people in this house then, and Rory Angus was living on the next farm, the one that's vacant now. He was the one that could play the fiddle and make you dance, if it was dancing you were after. And when we'd have the milling frolics at Johnnie Hughie's, that's when we wouldn't get home till seven in the morning." When, in the reverie of recollection, the old woman smiles contentedly and her husband chuckles jovially, it becomes obvious that the folk-culture imported by the settlers has played a much more important role in their lives than that of mere entertainment.

5

The Old Tradition Flourishes

HIGHLAND FOLKWAYS were, as we have seen, well suited to transmit traditional literature and music, but they also encouraged the making of new songs and new music. The stresses of pioneering life gave impetus to the composition of songs which were similar to the traditional lyrics composed in Scotland in that they were impromptu and dealt with personal experiences, but which were new in that they commented upon the unfamiliar process of migration. Naturally enough, the sentiments of such songs, even when the singer's tone is light-hearted, are deeply rooted. In reference to his songs of emigration, a Highlander will quote the homely proverb: "Is trom geum ba air a h-aineol." (Deep is the lowing of a cow on unfamiliar land.) The ludicrous element in the analogy should not, however, disguise the fact that the exile's song is a product of a genuinely felt emotion.

The career of the Bard MacLean offers a striking instance of the manner in which such poetry is evoked. In Scotland he had lived a comfortable life of ease and dignity in the tiny island of Tiree; having a gift for versifying he was appointed by the laird of Coll as his family bard. His house and his income were assured for life. Yet at the age of thirty-two he was lured by the promise of unclaimed land to set out for Nova Scotia.[1] How bitterly he was disappointed we have learned already from the passages quoted from his *Song to America*. Sadder or more heart-felt lines were seldom penned by poet than those with which the poem concludes:

> Tha mulad diomhair an deigh mo lionadh
> Bho'n 's eiginn striochdadh an seo ri m' bheo
> Air bheag toilinntinn 's a' choille chruim seo
> Gun duine faighneachd an seinn mi ceol.

Cha b' e sin m' abhaist an tus mo laithean;
'S ann bhithinn rabhartach aig gach bord,
Gu cridheil sunndach an comunn cuirteil,
A' ruith ar n-uine gun churam oirnn.[2]

A hidden grief has overfilled me since I've been doomed to stagnate here for the rest of my life with little amusement in this gnarled forest and without anyone to ask me if I'd sing a song.

That was not my custom in the early days; then I used to be frolicking at every table, happy and contented among cultured companions, passing the time without any care.

As he continued in the new land, his dissatisfaction slowly vanished; he found that there were compensations for his change of environment. He began to mingle with his pioneering neighbours and felt as much pleasure in their kitchens as he had at the aristocratic tables of the Highland lairds and chieftains in Scotland. His attitude towards life became more serious, and he turned his poetic ability to the composing of hymns as well as secular pieces.[3] When he died in 1848 one of his Highland companions in Nova Scotia wrote an elegy on his death which reveals the extent to which the once dissatisfied Bard had succeeded in adapting himself to the life and society of the New World:

Bu tu 'n riaraiche dibhe
Nuair bhiodh d' aoidhean 'n an suidhe;
'S gheibht' na h-orain bu ghrinne
Gu ro-phongail bho d' bhilibh;
Bha thu cliuiteach mar fhilidh
Measg nan Gaidheal 's gach ionad;
Dh' fhag do bhas iomad cridhe fo bhron.

Bha thu eolach 's a' Bhiobull—
Thug thu tlachd bho do chridh' dha;
'S iomadh laoidh rinn thu sgriobhadh
Ann am briathraibh ro-bhrigheil
Gu ar stiuradh 's an t-sligh' sin
A chaidh fhosgladh le Iosa
Le fhuil luachmhoir, do rioghachd na gloir'.[4]

You were a generous dispenser when your guests were seated around, and the loveliest songs would flow smooth from your lips; you were renowned as a poet among Highlanders everywhere; your death left many a heart in sorrow.

You were deeply versed in the Bible and gave it the affection of your heart, and many a hymn you wrote with words of deep meaning to guide us on that way to the kingdom of glory which was revealed by Jesus through his precious blood.

The Bard might have come to be considered a classic exponent of the pioneer life which has formed this continent, if he had composed his songs in English rather than in his native Gaelic. But if he had expressed himself in English, he might not have performed so well. The characteristics that give his poetry charm and vigour are an inheritance from the traditional Gaelic folk-song. His themes are simple, everyday events—a death, a Highland ball, an election, a raffle, the struggles of the temperance movement. His statements are direct, and his expressions are not decorated with the classic draperies that contemporary English poets found so convenient to borrow when their own invention faltered.

His peculiarly Gaelic style is characteristic, in greater or less degree, of the other immigrant Gaelic poets who composed on this side of the Atlantic, although few of them, even if fairly well educated, had MacLean's traditional bardic training, and still fewer had his originality. The majority were simple country farmers and fishermen who were moved to express their feelings in the form of poetry; and usually, like the Bard MacLean, they came to praise their new way of life rather than dispraise it. The settlers may have been loath to leave Scotland, yet their poetry shows that they soon learned to appreciate the advantages of their new home land. Even the humblest and most illiterate songster among them, no matter how unimaginative his language and how limited his vocabulary, seems to have found some pleasure and quiet amusement in the daily events of his active, outdoor life.

Although John MacLean was probably the most versatile and renowned of the Highland poets to come out to the New World, he was not the first or the only one. John MacRae of Kintail, whose Gaelic song composed after his arrival in the seventeen-seventies has already been quoted, preceded MacLean by almost half a century; but, imprisoned during the American Revolution for siding with the English cause in North Carolina, he suffered a miserable death before he had an opportunity to attune his lyre to the new climate.[5] Another Gaelic poet, the Reverend James MacGregor, was sixty years old and had been ministering to the people of Pictou County for over thirty years when the

Bard MacLean reached Nova Scotia in 1819. An active missionary and educator, he prepared a new translation of the Psalms of David in metre and published a volume of Gaelic hymns composed during journeys through his trackless and boundless territory. He hoped through the medium of these hymns to explain the principles of religion to his ill-informed countrymen,[6] and he was not disappointed in his aspiration, for Highlanders on both sides of the Atlantic welcomed his work, even though they never adopted it with the same enthusiasm which they bestowed on the hymns of their beloved Peter Grant. MacGregor's scholarly zeal may be said to have exceeded his artistic instinct; however sound his theology, it is not always expressed with the elegant simplicity of the unpretentious hymnist of Strathspey. His hymns went through several printings, however, and are still relished by the Gaels of the Old and the New World.

The same passion which typifies the work of the poets who succeeded MacGregor in the new land appears in the two surviving songs composed by him—one, a song in praise of the chieftain of his clan, and the other, a song in praise of a girl whom he left behind him in Scotland. Probably he never expected that these would be printed, but their contents were dear to his heart none the less, for he wrote them both in his neat handwriting on vacant pages of his still extant copy of a Gaelic song-book.[7] We can sympathize with the loneliness of his unmarried state when we read his glowing praises of his loved one far away:

> Gur mise bheir gradh gu brath do'n chailin
> A dh' fhag mi sealan am dheidh;
> Tha aice os chach gach agh 's gach barrachd,
> Mar aille gealaich measg reul.
> 'S i seamh-osag fhann an t-samhraidh choibhneil
> Bheir gleann us coille fo bhlath;
> 'S le dubh-neoil a' gheamhraidh 's anrath gaillinn
> Chan annsa fanail r' a sgath.

I shall cherish forever a love for the girl whom I left behind me a short time ago; she possesses a glory and virtue above all others, like the beauty of the moon among stars. She is the light-winged breeze of gentle summer bringing warmth to glen and to forest; the dark clouds of winter and the gloom of the snow-storm will not linger when she is near.

The romance had a prosaic ending;[8] his "light-winged breeze" was not attracted by the prospects of a pioneer's life. Instead, she made a comfortable marriage in Scotland. The disappointed poet decided to choose as a wife someone of less ethereal qualities. He selected a young lady in Halifax whom he scarcely knew but who was very highly recommended by his friends. He was too busy to go a-wooing, so he wrote her a letter of proposal and had to engage a friend to ride with it to her from Pictou, for in 1796 there was no postal service in the country. The young lady accepted. MacGregor ordered a new suit of clothes to be prepared for him at Halifax, arrived there on a Monday, dirty and tired after travel, and put up at an inn. He did not wish to call on his bride-to-be until he was properly dressed for the occasion; and since his new clothes were not ready on time, he did not see her until Tuesday evening immediately before the wedding ceremony. After spending a day in Halifax receiving friends, the young couple rode off through the woods on Thursday, and the busy minister returned to his duties at Pictou.

While MacGregor is best remembered for his labours as missionary, minister, and educator, those who read his poetry will recognize the true Gael, devoted alike to religion, to clanship, and to love.

When he died in 1830, another young Highlander, Duncan Black Blair, was just maturing in Scotland and preparing to follow in his steps as clergyman and bard in Nova Scotia.[9] While Duncan was still young, his father, a shepherd, had found employment in some of the most beautiful parts of the Highlands. Perhaps because this scenery awakened the young lad's appreciation for nature, he became an able poet. After studying for the ministry in Edinburgh and gaining his licence he went to Nova Scotia. In 1848 he was called to the charge of Barney's River and Blue Mountain, and there he remained until his death. Although he had neither the breadth of inspiration of the Bard MacLean nor the religious profundity of MacGregor, his poetry has vigour and charm. And he has to his credit[10] the unusual distinction of composing a poem on Niagara Falls which does justice to the majesty of the theme.

A Thi mhoir a chruthaich na duilean
'S a shocraich an cruinne
Le d' ghairdean cumhachdach, neartmhor
Air a bhunait,
Is glormhor an obair a rinn thu,
Niagara ainmeil,
An t-eas mor a rinn thu chumadh
'S an t-seann aimsir.

Siud an t-eas iongantach, loghmhor,
Eas mor na gairich,
Eas ceothranach, liath-ghlas na smuidrich,
'S na buirich ghabhaidh;
Eas fuaimearra, labhar na beucail,
A' leum 'n a steallaibh
Thar bhile nan creagan aosmhor
'N a chaoiribh geala.

O great Being who created the elements and established the universe upon its foundation with your mighty and all-powerful arms, majestic is that work which you formed—the renowned Niagara, the great waterfall which you carved out in ancient time.

Behold the stupendous and wondrous falls, the falls loud roaring, the mist-shrouded falls grey with vapour, thundering so awesomely; the falls crashing, resounding and bellowing, and welling and streaming over the lip of the age-old escarpment in sheets of white foam.

In his poetry we find none of the Bard MacLean's horror of the New World. He admits that the winter is cold but accepts it with cheerful resignation:

Anns a' gheamhradh neo-chaoin
Thig a' ghaoth le fead ghoineant',
'S bidh cruaidh ghaoir feadh nan craobh,
'S iad fo shraonadh na doininn.
Bidh sneachd trom air gach gleann,
'S cathadh teann mu gach dorus;
Ach bidh lon againn 's blaths,
'S bidh sinn manranach, sona.[11]

In the surly winter the wind comes with its shrill whistle, and there's a loud moaning among the trees under the blast of the storm. There's deep snow in each valley and heavy drifts around every door; but we have food and warmth, and we're companionable and contented.

The tradition of composing poetry survived the passing of the first settlers and was perpetuated by their descendants. In their

songs the somewhat reluctant admiration of the new environment noticeable in the work of Duncan Blair is displaced by an
unqualified devotion to it, reminiscent of the praise of mountain
and stream so common in the nature poetry composed in Scotland. As Neil MacLeod said of the Highland emigrants:

> Ged chaidh an sgapadh air gach taobh,
> Cha chaochail iad an gnaths.[12]

Although they were scattered in every direction, they did not change
their ways.

The work of Malcolm Gillis of Cape Breton, which has acquired a certain degree of fame, is typical in this respect. The
most celebrated of all his songs, one called *Am Braighe* (The
Brae),[13] derives its inspiration from the beauty of the hill on
which he lived, from the pleasantness of his neighbours, and
from the happiness of the country life he led.

Gillis is representative of most of the New World poets both
in upbringing and in outlook.[14] He was born in South-West
Margaree in 1856. His ancestors were Catholic Highland emigrants from Morar. He picked up what education he could in the
local country school and afterwards served several years as a
country school-teacher. He taught himself how to play the fiddle,
the bagpipes, and the organ. He carried a vast store of traditional tunes in his memory, and composed some tunes of his own to
suit his songs. He was devoted to his native Margaree and its
Gaelic-speaking inhabitants:

> Chan eil aite 'n diugh fo'n ghrein
> 'S am b' fhearr leam fhein bhith tamhachd
> Na Braigh' na h-Aibhne measg nan sonn
> O'm faighte fuinn na Gaidhlig.[15]

There's no place under the sun today where I would rather stay than
on the slopes of the river among the worthies where the melodies of
Gaelic can be heard.

On one occasion he taught school at Cheticamp, an Acadian
French settlement in Cape Breton. Although he was no more
than thirty miles distant from his beloved "Brae," he felt dis-

contented both with the people and with the surroundings.[16] He
heard no Gaelic, nothing but French:

> Ann an comunn cha chluinn mi
> Orain bhlasd' agus fuinn orr';
> 'S ged is tric a' dol cruinn iad,
> Cha bhruidhnear a' Ghaidhlig
>
> Ach Fraingis nach b' eol dhomh,
> 'S nuair a labhras iad comhla,
> Cha tuig ach fear eolach
> Gur e comhradh th' aig pairt dhiubh.
>
> Nuair a choinnicheas rium gruagach
> 'S a labhras mi sugrach,
> 'S ann a fhreagras i mugach
> "Bon jour," no "Belle soirée."

In company I never hear sweet songs and their melodies; and although they often gather, they don't speak Gaelic but French, which
I don't know; and when they're talking together no one but a sage
could tell that it's a conversation they're having. When a girl meets
me and I speak very sweetly to her, then she answers boorishly
"Bon jour" or "Belle soirée."

In his estimation nature had endowed Cheticamp much less
generously than his home land:

> Chan eil moran gu m' mhiann ann,
> Chan eil seorsa de dh' ian ann
> Ach faoileagan fiadhaich
> Bhios a' sgiathadh thar saile.
>
> Ann am maduinn ghil, shamhraidh,
> Cha chluinn mi guth smeoraich
> No lon dubh air barr mheoirean
> Toirt ciuil dhuinn mar b' abhaist.
>
> Coille charraigeach gun chroinn innt'
> Agus roinn bharr a buinn dhi:
> Craobh bheithe no uinnsinn
> Cha chuimhneach leam fas ann.
>
> Chan eil measan air mheoirean
> No cnomhan air calltuinn
> Mar bu lionmhor 's na beanntan
> Air am b' eolach a bha mi.

There's little to my liking here. There's no kind of bird here except wild gulls winging over the sea. On a bright summer morning I hear not the voice of the thrush, nor the blackbird on the branches such as I used to hear, carolling for us. Burly trees with no straight timber among them, and many of them uprooted; but I don't remember any birch or ash trees growing here. There's no fruit on the branches, no nuts on the hazel, such as there were so profusely in the hills I used to know.

This partisan devotion to the native soil could be illustrated by countless Gaelic songs of varying literary merit. One of the most instructive is that composed by a certain Donald Mac-Donald.[17] To understand the background, one must remember that the Highlanders who came to the new land were accustomed to a ready access to the sea or lake for fishing. Consequently the concessions of land which were taken up first were those convenient to the water. Settlers who arrived too late to acquire these prized shore locations had to content themselves with the remote and often precipitous rear-lands, but although forced to settle there by necessity rather than choice, they and their descendants came to love the mountain fastnesses. Donald Mac-Donald was one of this group. His parents came from Moidart to Cape Breton and settled on a mountain top in what is known as "the rear" of South-West Margaree.

Here in 1830 Donald was born, and here he was raised. Although he never went to school, he managed to teach himself to read both English and Gaelic. In later years he had to leave the "rear" and work for a season at "the shore," as the rival area was called. Here he found life, nature, and the people different from what he had known out back, and in every respect distinctly inferior. His prompt response was to compose a song, *Moladh a' Chuil agus Di-moladh a' Chladaich* (Praise of the Rear and Dispraise of the Shore). In the song he explains that he does not belong to the shore:

Cha b' ann thogadh mi as m' oig
Ach cul nam morbheann fiachail' ud
Far an goireadh riabhag 's smeorach
Maduinn or-bhuidh', ghrianachail.

'S ann do'n chul thug mise run,
'S gu'n duraiginn bhith 'n comhnuidh ann,
Far am fas a' choille dhluth,

> Gu slatach, lubach, meoireanach;
> I cho dubhghorm, maothbhog, sughmhor,
> 'S duilleach ur 'g a comhdachadh;
> Faileadh cubhraidh thar gach flur
> Th' air feadh nan lub 's nan sronagan.

It wasn't here that I was raised as a boy but in the rear among those lofty, stately mountains where the lark and the robin sing on sunny golden mornings.

It's the rear I gave my affection to, and it's there I'd like to be always where the dense forest grows with its supple branches and twigs—the forest that is so deep green and soft and pithy when the new leafage covers it, and the fragrance rises from all the trails and groves.

He makes it entirely clear to the "bunch of fishermen," as he calls his new neighbours, that their mode of life and their environment offer none of the attractions of the life he used to know.

Though the satiric vehemence of the poet's special pleading probably reflects a genuinely intense allegiance to his home soil, his bantering tone suggests that he is willing to accept a retort; and this retort was provided, in the traditional manner of a medieval flyting, by Duncan MacLellan[18] in a song, inevitably called *Moladh a' Chladaich agus Di-moladh a' Chuil* (Praise of the Shore and Dispraise of the Rear). Actually, although Duncan's wife was a shore-dweller, the poet himself had no claim to the title, since he lived in the Margaree valley quite near Donald's own home; but he argues the case as if he were a fisherman and with apparent seriousness sweeps the protagonist's claims aside. He assures us that a visit to Donald's country will soon dispel any false impression we may have gained from Donald's song:

> Chi thu coille ghoirid, cham,
> Mu'n cuairt air sgall de chlireadh ann,
> 'S ma chaidh a threabhadh leis a' chrann,
> Chan eil am fonn 'g a innseadh dhuinn.

You'll see stumpy, crooked trees surrounding a bald patch of clearing, and if it was ever turned with a plough, the appearance of the ground wouldn't tell you so.

He belittles every attraction that the rival poet had adduced. Donald had praised the beautiful flowers of the rear; Duncan unceremoniously disposes of them:

Nuair a thig an geamhradh duint',
Ged 's math na flurain, crionaidh iad;
'S mor gu'm b' fhearr bhith 'n taic an t-sail'
Far 'm faicte traigh us lionadh leat
Na cumail suil air duilleach dluth
Air feadh nan lub 's nan leanagan.

When the winter closes in, the flowers will wither, although they're
fine; I'd far rather be beside the sea and watch the ebb and flow than
be staring at dense leafage among the groves and meadows.

He enumerates the advantages of the fisherman's environment
and concludes with the good-natured wish that Donald will still
be willing to visit his adversary on the shore.

Praise of his home land was an inexhaustible theme for the
New World bard. Humour came close behind among the favourite themes. Humour is not a quality that can be analysed very
satisfactorily or, indeed, even described, and Gaelic humour is
particularly elusive. Any Gael will assure you that it is impossible to translate a joke from his language into English. But
one might venture to describe the humour of the Gael, at least
as we find it in his songs, as a sly chuckle on the part of the bard
at the expense of some human failing either in himself, or more
often in someone else. There is nothing wild or grotesque or sudden
about a Gaelic humorous song; there is no "punch line" to it;
it is the very antithesis of the modern radio comedian's style of
humour. Perhaps it is more akin to the quiet and subtle humour
of the French, who seem to find their amusement in the observation and description of mankind.

No quotation can demonstrate the peculiar charm of a Gaelic
humorous song. It belongs to its setting; it has no claims to
universal appeal, but is composed for one neighbourhood and
one situation. A brief sample of typical themes might give some
idea of the bard's method and art. James MacIsaac of Mira loses
his favourite red rooster to a hawk; the result, *Oran a' Chlamhain*
(Song of the Hawk).[19] Archie J. MacKenzie of Christmas Island
takes the priest's advice and leaves the state of bachelordom;
the result, a song, *Aideachadh an Fhleasgaich Ghlic* (Confession
of a Wise Bachelor), in which he helplessly narrates the troubles
he has endured during his unmarried days.[20] MacDougall shoots
a bear; the result, Allan MacDonald of South-West Margaree

composes a song, *Oran a' Mhathain* (Song of the Bear), in which the brother of the slain bear confesses his terror of the savage hunters who are out on his trail.[21] The list could be increased indefinitely, for the settlers and their children were quick to see a joke in the simple events of their daily life, and the bards were just as ready to embody the comedy of life in song.

At times the Highlander would revert from the good-natured song of humour to the satire that had been so dear to the hearts of the bards in Scotland. The satire of the Gael, like his humour, is inspired by the failings of human beings; but, unlike his humour, it is stinging, biting, and often downright offensive. The Gaelic language seems to be particularly suited to poetry of this type. One of the Gaelic bards of Cape Breton confesses, "I always use English when I'm composing poetry unless it's satire I'm writing. Then I use the Gaelic; there's no other language that can express what I want to say so well, when I really want to scorch someone."

The language of the best of these satires is so violent that, perhaps fortunately, they have not been recorded, and since the satirist's art is now suffering decay it is unlikely that many specimens of the type can be recovered. But any well-informed Gael can mention the names of at least two or three satirists he has known, perhaps at times to his own cost. And local histories are copiously supplied with the names of others. One of the most remarkable, to judge from his record, must have been Hugh Og MacLean.[22] While he was living at Sight Point (in Cape Breton) he found particular delight in composing insulting songs directed against his two neighbours, Allan Beag MacDonald and Sandy McLeod. All three were in other respects cordial friends; but Sandy had no relish for ridicule, and Allan Beag in particular was so very readily offended that whenever he heard a new satire directed against him, he would race over to Hugh's house and threaten the satirist's life. Ironically, Hugh was so facile that he was always able on the spur of the moment to compose a song complimentary to his enraged victim and thereby pacify him. But Hugh could not long resist his *penchant*. No sooner had Allan returned home satisfied than the restless bard would begin to meditate another satire. Finally Hugh and his two victims

moved away from Sight Point, each to a different part of Cape
Breton; and, according to the historian of Inverness County, the
sole reason for their separation was the rancour incited by the
satires of Hugh MacLean.

Though the bards were quick to ridicule the living in their
satires, they were always willing to eulogize the dead in their
elegies. If we make allowance for the exaggeration inherent in
both, the two genres, apparently so antithetical, when considered
in conjunction actually provide a fairly coherent portrait of the
private lives of the pioneers.

The elegies recall on the one hand the stern piety of their way
of life. In extolling James MacDonald of Cape Breton, who died
prematurely in Halifax while studying for the ministry, his
elegist remarks:

> Labhradh e gu dana
> Ri luchd dubh na ceilidh Shabaid,
> Mur a sguradh iad 'n a thrath dheth,
> Gu'n gairmeadh Satan dhachaidh iad.[23]

> He would boldly tell the wicked Sabbath breakers that, if they
> didn't stop in time, Satan would call them home.

The elegies remind us on the other hand of the pioneers' warm,
human affections. The severance of true friendship has seldom
found more pathetic utterance than in the lament composed by
the Bard MacLean in Nova Scotia when he learned that his
chieftain and patron, the laird of Coll, had died.[24] The poem
possesses a peculiar melancholy in that it is said to be the last
of its kind, the last lament composed by a family bard for his
chieftain; and the poet's obvious sincerity makes it doubly
melancholy:

> Thainig sgeul thar nan cuantan
> Mheudaich mulad us gruaim dhomh le bron;
> Chuir e m' inntinn gu gluasad,
> 'S iomadh aon dha 'n do dh' fhuasgail e deoir:
> Gu'n robh 'n t-Alasdair priseil
> Air a chaireadh gu h-iosal fo'n fhoid
> Ann an leaba na h-urach,
> Ann an suain as nach duisg e le ceol.

Over the ocean came news which painfully stirred my grief and gloom; it set my mind to pondering and drew the tears of many a person—the news that the dear laird, Alexander, had been buried deep under the sod on an earthy bed, in a sleep from which no music will ever awaken him.

A vision swims before his eyes of the funeral barge landing on the shore which he remembers so well:

> Nuair a chunnacas do bhata
> Tigh'nn gu Rudha na h-Airde fo sheol,
> 'S iomadh aon a bha craiteach
> Thu bhith d' shineadh fo chlaraibh air bord.
> Cha bu shunndach an fhailte
> Bh' aig do mhuinntir a' fasgadh nan dorn;
> 'S iomadh cuimhneachan cairdeil
> Bh' aca 'n oidhch' ud mu'n armunn nach beo.

When your boat was seen coming under sail to High Point, many is the one who lamented that you should be lying aboard her stretched out under the planks. Your people were wringing their hands, and there was no cheer in their greeting. Many were their affectionate memories that night of the chieftain no longer alive.

After enumerating the fine qualities of the deceased laird, he salutes the heir to the estate and vows his allegiance to him in those final stanzas of the poem which show that thirty-six years of separation by the wide waters of the Atlantic had in no way lessened his affection for the land and people he left behind him:

> Mur biodh gainnead mo storais,
> Phillinn fhathast air m' eolas a null
> Gus an ruiginn an t-aite
> Far 'n do shuidhich thu larach as ur.
> Cha bhiodh eagal gu brath dhomh
> Fhad 's a bhiodh tu laidir ri m' chul.
> (B' fhearr gu'n robh mi gun d' fhagail!)
> Gheibhinn fasgadh fo sgaile do chuit.

If it weren't for my lack of wealth, I'd journey back even now to the land I remember until I reached the place where you have established the house anew. Not a care would I have so long as your power was supporting me. (Would that I had never left you at all!) Under the shelter of your realm I'd find protection.

Every imaginable occasion gave rise to verse among the Gaels in the New World. The resulting poems were occasionally printed in little booklets, but the majority of the songs, including even the best of them, were not written down but were composed in the bard's mind and, like the folklore that the Gaels brought with them from Scotland, passed on from mouth to mouth. It would be impossible to produce a complete inventory of the poetry composed in the new land by the Gaelic bard; his method of composing is too rapid and elusive. In Gaelic, he would never say, "*Sgriobh* mi oran," "I *wrote* a song," but rather "*Rinn* mi oran," "I *made* a song." Murdoch Morrison of Ferguson's Lake, Cape Breton, is a case in point. Two dozen of his songs were collected and published by one of the poet's admirers.[25] But his acquaintances complain that the collection gives the reader no real idea of his ready riming wit. He called at a house one day and stayed for dinner. While he was eating, the lady of the house saw that his cap was very ragged, and so without drawing attention to what she was doing, she patched it up. When the bard noticed the repairs as he was about to leave, without so much as a pause for breath he poured out a song in praise of his thoughtful hostess.

Music also flourished. Each district had its fiddler and piper who could compose new melodies as well as play the repertoire brought from the Old Land. To an even greater extent than the songs composed in the New World, however, this new music has been lost without being recorded. One collection of violin music composed by Cape Breton Gaels was published in 1940,[26] and the fact that it contains the work of sixteen different composers proves that the musical genius of the people has not been mute, especially when we consider that the collection represents only the works of living composers, and they for the most part men from only one of the four counties of the island.

The quantity of songs and music composed by the pioneers is, of course, no guarantee of excellence. The aesthetic quality of their folk-literature and folk-music, both traditional and newly composed, varies as much as that of any comparable folk-culture. Comparison with the attainments of more complex non-oral cultures is of dubious significance. The folk-poet and folk-musician do not address themselves to an audience fit, but few. There once had been a time in Scotland when trained Gaelic bards had composed recondite poems that could hardly have been understood by the entire populace; but in the New World, unless a song appealed to the fancy of the ordinary settler, its chances of transmission were slight. Hence the surviving poetry and music have been moulded by the canons of taste shared by the majority of the people for whom the artists composed; and herein consists the chief merit of their folk-art. It is universally popular, immediately understandable, and functionally related to the settlers' way of life.

6

~~~~~~

Gaelic in Print

THE MAJORITY of the Gaels who settled in the New World could not, it is true, read their own language; they were accustomed and even contented to rely on oral transmission for their literary recreation. But in the new environment some of the more enterprising of their descendants ventured to publish Gaelic writings; and even those Gaels who had up to this time been illiterate received these publications with enthusiasm, although they had to puzzle out the spelling slowly and painfully as best they could until they acquired a self-taught mastery of the reading of their language.

The quantity of Gaelic pamphlets, papers, and books published in North America is considerable and somewhat astonishing.[1] The usual publication of this type was intended for only a small reading public, and only a very few copies, therefore, were issued. The earliest of these publications are by now excessively scarce, and many items have, without a doubt, perished unrecorded. The identity of the first Gaelic publication issued in North America must, for this reason, remain undecided. We know that the Provincial Congress of North Carolina in 1776 resolved to publish a declaration in Gaelic. Somewhat incomprehensibly, the Highland settlers in the area had supported King George against the American revolutionists. Their forces were defeated and captured, and the Congress wished to notify the prisoners' "unhappy families and connections" that "every indulgence which humanity and compassion can give" would be extended to those in their power, but with a warning that their treatment of the prisoners would depend upon "the future good behaviour of those who still remain in the Province."[2] Whether the translation of the resolution into Gaelic was ever made we do not know, but in any case North Carolina still establishes the record for having produced the first surviving Gaelic publication. The Reverend Dugald Crawford had delivered two sermons in Gaelic at Raft Swamp, and in the year 1791 they were printed at Fayetteville, North Carolina.[3] Probably other items appeared after that date from the local presses of this state where so many Highlanders had settled, but if they did, they have perished. The only other recorded publication is a new edition of Peter Grant's hymns which appeared in 1826, and after that date we hear no more from the state.

The Gaels who had settled further north—those in Nova Scotia, in Prince Edward Island, and in Ontario—were slower to begin publishing in their mother tongue, but when once they began, they persevered more loyally than their compatriots in the south. Like them they sanctified their undertaking by first issuing religious works. In 1832 we find a reprint appearing in Prince Edward Island of the Gaelic translation of a religious work for Protestants, Dyer's *Christ's Famous Titles*.[4] In 1836 editions of the hymns of Dugald Buchanan and Peter Grant were published in Montreal.[5] In 1841 the Catholics on Prince Edward Island republished Father Ronald Rankin's *Gaelic Manual*.[6]

The first known Gaelic book to be both written in the New World and published there is a modest little volume entitled *The Youth's Companion*. It was printed in Pictou, Nova Scotia, in 1836 under the Gaelic title, *Companach an Oganaich, no An Comhairliche Taitneach* (The Youth's Companion, or The Friendly Counsellor). The author, Alexander MacGillivray, belonged to a talented family.[7] His father, John the Piper, was born in Moidart and there was appointed by the laird of Glenaladale as family piper. John was something of a bard as well as a musician. He emigrated to Prince Edward Island and finally settled on the Gulf shore in Antigonish County.

Alexander, his son, was a real Highlander. He stood six foot five, and was large of mind as well as of body. He was a promising student and started to prepare for the priesthood, but his health was not equal to the requirements of the calling. He therefore tried to serve his neighbours by devoting his command

of the Gaelic language to the gathering together and translating
of timely reflections on the principal moral and spiritual issues
of life.

His book, *The Youth's Companion*, contains essays on a varied
range of topics, such as "Temperance, Wisdom, and Courage,"
"Women, Love, and Marriage," "Death and Eternity." Under
such inclusive headings each topic is discussed succinctly and
then amply illustrated from the writings of moralists and teachers
of many areas. François de Sales, St. Gregory, John Gerson, St.
Bernard, and Gobinett exhort the reader. Xenophon discusses
the education of children in Persia; St. Paul defines the duties
of a wife towards her husband; Sir Philip Sidney explains that
the desires of a truly good man are few.

The Youth's Companion is a pleasing book. It appeared at a
time when the young were in need of a guide, and in an environment where they might not easily find one. Nova Scotia was a
young and unruly country. The settlers were not notably
interested in the values of contemplation. Even in Halifax, the
capital city, where the governing classes of Nova Scotia lived,
there was at this period only one bookstore, the contents of
which, according to Captain Moorsom, reflected the mental level
of Halifax society. He found nothing in it but a catalogue of law-
books and school-books and a windowful of etchings and drawing
paper: "In vain do we inquire for some of those numberless
sheets printed for the instruction of the juvenile, or for the
standard works that assist in forming the more advanced mind;
none such are to be procured, except by express commission to
England; and the reason uniformly assigned is—'We should find
no sale for them.' "[8]

Despite this alleged indifference of Nova Scotians towards
didactic literature, Alexander MacGillivray's book won an appreciative audience among the Gaelic-speaking settlers in the
province. It apparently found its way into even the humblest
settler's cabin and appealed to the Highlanders, especially those
of the Catholic faith, for whom it was particularly intended.
Today, more than a hundred years since it was published, its
influence survives among men and women of Highland descent,

who, looking back to the days of their childhood, recall the time when they were inspired by its teaching. The appeal of his work may be explained, at least in part, by the fact that the author exercised a kindly tolerance towards the human failings of his neighbours. Under the heading of "Drunkenness," for instance, he rejoices that "this most pernicious and destructive vice is daily losing ground"; and he recommends to all his young countrymen that they should read the *Temperance Recorder* attentively; but he does not breathe a single rabid word about abstinence, and he willingly accords his readers the age-long privilege of enjoying a drink on Christmas Day.[9]

Alexander MacGillivray was devoted to his mother tongue, Gaelic. He was not under the obligation of rallying his country-men to the support of their native language, as the Gaelic writers who came after him were, for, at the time he was writing, the majority of his readers, especially those advanced in age, spoke Gaelic fluently and knew but little English. He was concerned, however, to encourage the younger generation to preserve the language of their forefathers in all its purity. In a lengthy foot-note he complains that an English word, "prisoner," has been adopted into the Gaelic language, as *priosanach*, and seems to be replacing the ancient native word *ciomaich* which should more correctly be used. The new mongrel word, he complains, is

> wholly derived from the English language, and is in general use among very enlightened men, as well as the common people of our country; not from any conviction of its being the proper, or literal Gaelic word, . . . but from the general prevailing custom of using foreign words in common conversation.
> This is a foul blot on the sacred antiquity of our mother tongue. . . . If such a custom be tolerated or much longer continued, the ancient Celtic shall be so polluted and confused that we shall have a new garbling dialect instead of that in which Ossian sung.[10]

We may judge from this instance that the author was interested not merely in the moral welfare of his fellow countrymen but also in the welfare of their mother tongue.

From the time of Alexander MacGillivray's work on, there is a steady trickle of original Gaelic writing published in the New World. In 1840 we hear of a Gaelic newspaper by the name of *Cuairtear na Coille* (The Forest Traveller)[11] appearing in Ontario; in 1850, another, by name *Am Fear-Teagaisg* (The Teacher).[12]

In 1851 the enterprising John Boyd of Antigonish, shortly after setting up the first printing press in the county, began to issue a monthly Gaelic magazine, entitled in English *The Gaelic Tourist*, and in Gaelic *An Cuairtear Og Gaelach*.[13] Already we begin to find examples of the manner in which the Highland spirit survived among the descendants of the Gaelic immigrants. John Boyd was a first generation Canadian by birth, but no one could have been more enthusiastically Highland in spirit. Apart from a little local news and a few locally composed songs and sketches, his paper was filled with extracts from the works of Scottish Gaelic writers, and the theme of the articles was generally Highland history and the glories of the ancient clans.

Such material evidently appealed to the readers. Writing in 1891 on the history of Antigonish, the Reverend Ronald Mac-Gillivray, a native of the county, recollects the delight with which this periodical was received. Although he was only five years old at the time that it was in circulation, he still remembers "the pleasure and delight the advent of the *Cuairtear*, month after n. nth, brought to the family." He recalls the scene in his household at its arrival: "When the *Cuairtear* arrived this evening, the neighbours gathered in, the candles were lit, and the old man began to read out its contents from the first to the last page, while the audience listened to its tales, songs and stories with the most intense interest and pleasure."[14]

But times were changing. By now many of the younger people in Antigonish County had acquired English and no longer took any great interest in the language of their parents. In the year 1852 John Boyd attempted to satisfy the changing tastes of his readers by issuing a weekly newspaper, *The Casket*. Half of this new publication was devoted to songs, stories, and editorials written in Gaelic, just as they had been in his earlier paper. But the news section of the paper, which contributed the other half to the total contents, was written in English. The editor explained to his former Gaelic supporters that they would probably find the new form of the paper more convenient and pleasant than the old *Gaelic Tourist* had been.[15] And shortly after the *Casket* got under way, he confessed that the Gaelic language seemed to be yielding place to English very rapidly:

> Tha sinn duilich gu'm feum sinn aideach gu'm bheil a' Ghaidhlig a' tarruing air ais a h-uile latha agus a' Bheurla a' deanamh a bonnaibh na's treasa us na's treasa a h-uile car; air chor 's gu'm bheil a h-uile coltas air gu'n cuir i 'Ghaelig bhochd an cuil chumhann mur faigh i 'chobhair ach mar tha i faotainn.[16]

> We're sorry that we must admit that Gaelic is drawing back every day and English strengthening her foundations more and more at every turn; so that there is every appearance that she will put the poor Gaelic into a tight corner unless it gets more support than it is getting.

John Boyd's prediction was correct; Gaelic was driven into a tight corner in the county, although the language still survives among some of the people of Highland stock there today, almost a hundred years after Boyd's first cry of alarm. The Gaelic section of his paper was gradually reduced in size and eventually disappeared as a regular feature.

The next Gaelic publication of importance to appear in the New World was founded in Toronto, Ontario. The editor, Angus Nicholson, was eager to see more emigrants come from Scotland to take possession of the opening resources of Canada. At first he edited an English paper which carried occasional Gaelic columns, *Albannach Chanada: The Canada Scotsman*. In 1871 he brought out the first number of a new publication, *An Gaidheal* (The Gael), which was devoted entirely to material of interest to Highlanders. He had agents spread through North America to seek out subscribers among the scattered Gaelic settlements. The list of agencies is interesting, for it shows us how widely spread the settlers had now become:

> Ontario: Durham, Sullivan, Williamstown, Bulmer's Island, South
>   Finch, Rothsay.
> Quebec: Lingwick, Stornoway, Winslow, Lake Megantic.
> New Brunswick: Dalhousie, Black Sand.
> Nova Scotia: Springville, Pictou, River Denys.
> Prince Edward Island: Charlottetown, Orwell, Wood Island.
> Michigan: Lake Linden.
> Illinois: Chicago.
> North Carolina: Lumberton.

Shortly after the first number of *An Gaidheal* appeared, Angus Nicholson was appointed Dominion emigration agent,[17] and since his work required him to live in Scotland, he shifted his publishing headquarters from Toronto to Glasgow. Although the paper continued to circulate in Canada and the United States, it became to all intents and purposes a Scottish publication and therefore irrelevant to the history of Gaelic writing produced in North America.

In the last quarter of the nineteenth century Gaelic publishing found support, independent of Scotland, in two men, both Canadians by birth but Gaels by inclination, who were filled with a zeal to record in print as much as possible of the language which they loved so dearly. They both fought against the growing indifference of their fellow Gaels in the New World towards the language and culture of their ancestors. They both struggled against financial odds in order to keep their publications going. They both laboured to recover and put in print the Gaelic songs which were in their time still circulating by word of mouth among their friends. One of these men was the Reverend Alexander Maclean Sinclair;[18] the other, Jonathan G. MacKinnon.

Although born in Glenbard, Antigonish County, in 1840, Alexander Sinclair was closely connected with Gaelic Scotland. His mother was the daughter of the Bard MacLean and had emigrated with her father from Tiree in 1819 at the age of nine. His father John Sinclair had emigrated from Sutherland in 1832. The child had been named Alexander in memory of the Bard's patron Alexander MacLean, the laird of Coll, and was reared in an atmosphere of Gaelic music and poetry and tradition. Although the Bard's death occurred when Alexander Sinclair was only eight years old, he retained an affectionate memory of his grandfather; in fact, according to a traditon held by one branch of the family, he gave himself the middle name Maclean out of respect for the Bard and the clan.

Mr. Sinclair became a Presbyterian clergyman and held charges first in Pictou County and then in Prince Edward Island. In his profession he met many of the best-informed Gaels in Canada. He also made a tour of Scotland and spent some time in Tiree gathering information about his grandfather. Moreover, he inherited from the Bard two valuable manuscript volumes of Gaelic poetry.[19] One of these was a collection gathered by Dr. Hector MacLean of Tobermory in Mull about 1768 which Samuel Johnson had examined when he visited the island in 1773. In it Dr. Hector had recorded many classic Gaelic poems. When the Bard got the manuscript, he added on unused sheets many of his own compositions. The other volume inherited by Dr. Sinclair was a collection of Gaelic songs and classical poems recorded by the Bard while he was living in Scotland.

Much of the manuscript material had never appeared in print, and it was to the task of preserving this rich body of literature and making it accessible to the public that Dr. Sinclair first turned his attention. At the same time he collected songs indefatigably from his Gaelic friends in Canada. He commenced publishing in 1880 and continued until 1904.[20] He brought out *Clarsach na Coille* (The Harp of the Forest), which contained the bulk of the Bard MacLean's secular compositions, as well as songs by other authors; a collection of hymns by the Bard and others; an anthology entitled *The Glenbard Collection*; four volumes known as *The Gaelic Bards*, containing selections from poets arranged chronologically from 1411 to 1875; two volumes of poetry composed by various members of the Clan MacLean; two miscellaneous volumes of Gaelic songs, *Filidh na Coille* (The Forest Poet) and *MacTalla nan Tur* (Echo of the Towers); an edition of John Lom MacDonald's poetry; and one of Alexander MacKinnon's. He busily wrote articles on Highland lore for periodicals. And, being a true Highlander, he was intensely interested in genealogy, especially in the details of the clan to which he was so closely related, the Clan MacLean. He wrote several small booklets on genealogical matters and one large volume, *The Clan Gillean, or History of the MacLeans*.

Rigorously trained editors of the present age might be a little shocked at the liberties Dr. Sinclair took with the songs he published.[21] Sometimes he rearranged them in a more artistic form than that in which he had found them. He disliked grammatical irregularities and always tried to smooth out any in the poetry he published. But his methods are excusable, since he was dealing with orally transmitted poetry at a period when oral tradition, no longer vigorous, was prone to lapses of memory.

Whether Dr. Sinclair was faithful to the letter of his originals or not, he was certainly devoted to the spirit of them. Highlanders naturally admire their native body of poetry, but few would have been willing to undertake the labour of collecting and editing it and to shoulder the unrewarding financial burden of publishing it. Dr. Sinclair gave his time and energy enthusiastically to this cause, and the satisfaction he won was spiritual only. He prepared most of his editions from type columns already set up and printed in various local newspapers, and thereby eliminated the cost of type-setting; he gathered subscriptions from patriotic Gaels; yet he still could not clear expenses. In an appendix to one of his editions[22] he gives an accounting to his readers of the profit and the loss resulting from his various undertakings. He has lost about $86 on *Clarsach na Coille*, about $14 on *The Glenbard Collection*, about $88 on *MacTalla nan Tur*, and at the time of writing he expects to lose about $44 on *Filidh na Coille*. His profit has been $2 on the *Poems by John Lom MacDonald* and $26.14 on *The MacLean Bards!* He ruefully confesses that he feels very much like bidding farewell to the publishing of Gaelic books. We must not suppose Dr. Sinclair was mercenary; the fact, even though easily predictable, that it was difficult to convert an oral into a written culture was understandably discouraging to such an enthusiast. The mild bitterness of his remarks soon evaporated; two years later he brought out another volume of Gaelic poetry.

Dr. Sinclair's labours were remarkably valuable. He brought to light Gaelic songs that were previously available only to those who could inspect rare editions or manuscript collections. In the New World, where there were few Gaelic scholars competent to record the language in which local bards were daily composing, he gathered songs that would otherwise have been lost. He collected information about the settlers and their families which would now be irrecoverable.

The explanatory notes appended to the poetry Dr. Sinclair published, besides being useful to the literary historian, often have more than antiquarian value. His style is terse and concise but at the same time enlivened by a pungent individualism. As we read his comments we can readily picture the writer, tall, straight, and bearded, his exuberant mind charged with Gaelic wit and warmth and sparkle, yet balanced by that quality known as "Presbyterian common-sense." His remarks on the rebellion of 1715 are typical.[23] Unlike many Highlanders, who view this rising as a glorious and romantic episode of Scottish history, Dr. Sinclair heretically describes it as "a very ridiculous rebellion." "The truth is," he tells us, "that neither the Stewarts, descended from Mary Queen of Scots, nor the Georges were worth fighting for. There was not a man among them all fit to rule over a nation. Indeed the world could get along very well without any hereditary rulers." In the same direct vein, in 1881 he wrote concerning the emigration of the Highlanders to the New World: ". . . those who emigrated from Scotland are a great deal better off than the children of those who remained in that country of landlords and rents. It is a pity that all the crofters in the Highlands and Islands of Scotland could not be at once brought over to Manitoba."[24]

Although his publications lost him money, he must have been glad to recognize that his books made possible an understanding and appreciation of the little-known culture of the people to whom he belonged and whom he so much admired.

Jonathan G. MacKinnon was an equally outstanding contributor to the publication of Gaelic in the New World. He was born on the outskirts of Whycocomagh, a village with an Indian name but a Gaelic population, on the shores of the Bras d'Or Lakes in Cape Breton. The MacKinnons from whom he was descended had immigrated from the island of Skye in Scotland. As a young boy he was somewhat of an invalid and could not attend school regularly, but his mind was always active. While confined to the house he spent his time in acquiring information about his Gaelic forefathers. Eventually he managed to go to Sydney and attend the Academy, where he completed his high school studies. Here he found an opportunity to indulge an ambition he had always cherished. Even while bed-ridden in Whycocomagh, he had dreamed of producing a newspaper written entirely in Gaelic, the language which he heard in his home and which he loved. At the Sydney Academy he had his first taste of publishing, although not in Gaelic but in English, when he was appointed editor of the school paper.

With his great enthusiasm for the language and with the little experience he had acquired he summoned up courage to undertake the venture on which he had set his heart. He inserted an advertisement in the *Island Reporter* promising to publish a Gaelic newspaper if he could find a guarantee of support from five hundred subscribers. The five hundred names did not materialize, but "Jonathan G." (as he was commonly called) received letters from many enthusiastic Gaels, some of whom promised to find subscribers and others of whom offered to submit Gaelic material for publication providing he would undertake the venture.[25] Accordingly on May 28, 1892, he issued a small four-page paper in Sydney under the title of *Mac-Talla* (Echo), and he continued to produce a number once a week despite the prognostications of the pessimists that the undertaking would fail. Every word in the paper was in Gaelic, even the advertising, except when the language lacked a term to describe such current commodities as felt hats, stoves, molasses, and bicycles.

Although the young editor (he was only twenty-two) had undertaken the paper without any certainty that he would be able to continue it, it survived the first year. The yearly subscription price for the first volume was 50 cents. He enlarged the lay-out of the second volume to eight pages and increased the subscription price to $1. The paper was apparently going to prosper. During the third year of its career the subscription list rose to 1,100;[26] and later to 1,400.[27] But even this peak was hardly adequate to support the expenses of publication. In the seventh year of the paper (1899) some of the editor's close friends rallied around him and formed a printing and publishing corporation, issuing a thousand shares at $10 a share.[28] Prior to that time the editor had realized so little money from his endeavours that he was compelled to engage in part-time employment elsewhere in order to meet his expenses.

There were never sufficient subscribers, and some of those who did subscribe were very slow to pay. They were willing enough to have their names enrolled on the list, but once they began to receive the paper they absent-mindedly overlooked their part of the bargain. The editor used to print the names and addresses of those who were paying their subscriptions regularly under a column headed "Iadsan a phaigh" (Those who paid). One contributor suggested that the responsiveness of delinquent subscribers might be awakened by running a column headed "Iadsan nach do phaigh" (Those who didn't pay),[29] but the editor never ventured the experiment. He did, however, harry his readers frequently about payment. One angry subscriber was offended by the editor's reproaches levelled against unpatriotic Gaels. He composed a song in answer to these pleas for money and support, in which he compared the importunate *Mac-Talla* with the quiet and uncomplaining *Casket:*

> Tha mi 'n duil gu'm bheil e nar dhuit
> 'Bhith cur inisg air na Gaidheil
> Le bhith glaganach gun tamh
> Ag eigheach paidheadh a' *Mhic-Talla.*
>
> Faic an *Casket,* ∘ cho baidheil;
> Tha e modhail 's tha e samhach;
> Cha chluinn thu e 'g eigheach paidheadh—
> Cleas a' gharlaoich-ud *Mac-Talla.*
>
> Tha e corr us leth-chiad bliadhna
> Tighinn 'g ar n-ionnsuidh le deagh riaghailt,
> Us riamh am paidheadh cha do dh' iarr e—
> Cleas an spiocaire *Mac-Talla.*[30]

I consider that it's shameful for you to be reproaching the Gaels, ceaselessly prattling, shouting for payment for *Mac-Talla.*

Look at the *Casket,* so modest; it is mannerly and quiet; you never hear it shouting for payment—the trick of that rascal *Mac-Talla.*

More than half a century it's been coming to us in good order, and it has never asked for payment—the trick of that niggard *Mac-Talla.*

But the editor's pleas were necessary. In the tenth volume (1901-2) he was compelled to curtail the appearance of his paper from every week to every other week; Sydney had been ravaged by a serious fire, and the business men of the city had lost so severely that the paper's income from advertising was seriously depleted.[31] The paper continued to appear for two more volumes, but with the last number of the twelfth volume (June 24, 1904), the editor reluctantly confessed that he could no longer afford to continue publication. Sydney is located in the centre of a productive mining area, and, during the latter years of *Mac-Talla*'s career, the town experienced a great boom through the development of a steel company. The population of the town multiplied,[32] and prices soared correspondingly. The cost of production rose beyond the paper's income.[33] Mr. MacKinnon tells his readers in farewell:

> Air son *Mac-Talla* a chur a mach uair 's an da sheachdain cha b' fhuilear air a chuid bu lugha da mhile fear-gabhail a bhith aige. Dh' fhaodadh sin a bhith aige ged nach biodh ann de luchd-leughaidh Gailig ach na th' air eilein Cheap Breatuinn; ach nuair nach faighear an aireamh sin air fad us leud an t-saoghail, chan urrainnear tighinn gu co-dhunadh sam bith eile ach nach eil paipeir Gailig a dhith air na Gaidheil, gu bheil iad riaraichte le bhith comharraichte mar an aon chinneach Criosdail a th' air thalamh nach cosd ri paipeir a chumail suas 'n an cainnt fein.
> . . . na'm faigheamaid dearbhadh gu robh aireamh a dh' fhoghnadh de na Gaidheil iarrtach a chumail suas, bheireamaid ionnsuidh eile air. Ach gun dearbhadh no dochas, chan urrainn duinn ni eile dheanamh aig an am seo ach, le mor dhuilichinn, a leigeil bas.[34]

> In order to bring out *Mac-Talla* once every two weeks, it would require not less than two thousand subscribers. The paper could easily have that, even if there were no other Gaelic readers except those in Cape Breton; but when this number cannot be found throughout the length and breadth of the world, we can reach no other conclusion than that the Gaels do not want a Gaelic paper, and that they are content to be classed as the only Christian race in the world who will not pay to keep up a paper in their own language.
> . . . if we could find proof that an adequate number of Gaels were desirous of keeping it up, we should make another attempt. But with neither proof nor hope, we can do nothing else at this time except, with great regret, allow it to die.

No other entirely Gaelic periodical, even in Scotland, has run for so long as did *Mac-Talla*, and perhaps none has contained such varied material or appealed to a public so widespread. The subscription lists contain readers from every province of Canada, indeed from every quarter of North America—from Massachusetts and Michigan and North Dakota and California, from

Boston and New York and San Francisco, and even from Dawson in the Yukon;[35] from Scotland; and from New Zealand. One subscriber writes to the editor from Bangkok, Siam,[36] and another from Latitude 50° 59′ North, Longitude 19° West, on the high seas of the Atlantic.[37]

Although at first the material in the paper was limited to a few scraps of news and some Gaelic songs that had already appeared in print, the contents gradually became richer and more original. Contributors from Canada and Scotland sent in more and more new material which they had written or gathered expressly for the paper. Songs, especially, that had never before been recorded in print, came in from all directions.

The influence of these twelve plump volumes was more enduring than the small circulation list and the complaints of the editor might lead one to suspect. Although new subscribers did not clamour for copies, the paper was highly respected and loved. Perhaps only one copy went to a Gaelic settlement, but that is not to say that only one person read the paper there; young and old would gather around the local Gaelic scholars who could read the latest news and stories and songs from its pages. The copy would pass from household to household, and parents would teach their children to spell out the words of their mother tongue from its pages.

At a time when the Gaelic-speaking people were becoming ashamed of their own language, the paper elevated it in their eyes to a position of prestige. Jonathan G. MacKinnon had no cause to feel that his toils and trials had been in vain. Few men could have done more for the language and literature in the New World than he did, and only one—the Reverend A. Maclean Sinclair—did as much.

Jonathan G. did not cease to labour in the cause of Gaelic after he laid aside the old *Mac-Talla*. He made and published Gaelic translations of four literary classics;[38] and in 1928 he started to edit a small Gaelic monthly called *Fear na Ceilidh* (The Visitor), which ran for more than two years but then silently disappeared from circulation. He also conducted a Gaelic column in one of the Sydney newspapers for some years. Typically a Gael, he was deeply devoted to the island where he was born. He wrote and published a book—this time in English—on the early days of

Sydney,[39] the city about whose past history he had character-
istically become curious. He composed a Gaelic song in praise of
Cape Breton,[40] in which he tacitly reproaches his countrymen
for deserting the land of their birth in favour of distant cities
where they could earn more money:

> Far an d' fhuair mi m' arach og,
> Fanaidh mi le toil 's le deoin;
> Air cho fad 's gu'm bi mi beo,
> Cha dean an t-or mo mhealladh as.
>
> Eilean gorm nam beanntan ard,
> Tir mo dhuthchais, tir mo ghraidh;
> 'S iomadh tonn a bhuaileas traigh
> Mu'n iarr mi fath air carachadh.

Where I was reared as a boy, there I shall stay with delight and
pleasure; as long as I am living, gold will not tempt me away.

Verdant island of high mountains, land of my home, and land of my
love; many a wave will break on the shore before I'll seek a reason
to move away.

When he finally had to give up active life and go to the hospital, he was interrupted in a cherished undertaking—the preparation of a study on the Highland emigrations to Canada.[41] No
one could love and admire his fellow countrymen more than
Jonathan G. MacKinnon, although they have not all paid him
the debt of honour they owe him. In fact, they perhaps do not
realize its magnitude. When he died on January 13, 1944, at the
age of seventy-four, Gaels throughout the world lost a talented
exponent of their culture.

Other attempts have been made to run Gaelic periodicals in
the New World, but none so successful as the original *Mac-Talla*.
The Scottish Catholic Society of Canada sponsored a Gaelic
publication, *Mosgladh* (The Awakening); it appeared first in
magazine format in 1922 and was issued at irregular intervals for
five years; then it started up again in a more modest newspaper
format in 1928 and continued for another five years and more.
Its columns never attained the originality achieved by *Mac-
Talla* and were written only partly in Gaelic and quite extensively in English.

The late James MacNeil of Sydney, regretting that the Gaels
of the New World were not supporting a Gaelic newspaper of
their own, ventured to start one independently in 1925. He called

it *Teachdaire nan Gaidheal, or The Gaelic Herald*. It continued for ten years and more, but there were long and painful intervals between the appearance of the various numbers, so that the paper lost its continuity and presumably a good proportion of its paying adherents. About a year after beginning the paper the editor followed Jonathan G. MacKinnon's example and incorporated his paper with a thousand shares to be issued at $10 a share.[42] Whatever may have happened to the corporation, the paper itself eventually came to a standstill. James MacNeil also edited a Gaelic column in one of the Sydney papers, and he succeeded in preserving oral literature from extinction, although in common with other enthusiasts his labours brought him neither wealth nor fame.

The Gaels of Ontario have not equalled their brethren of the Maritimes in literary productivity, but at least they have the distinction of having provided a home to an able Gaelic writer and scholar, the late Dr. Alexander Fraser.[43] Born in the Highlands of Scotland, he came to Canada in 1886 at the age of twenty-six. He served at first as a newspaper-man and later became Archivist of the Province of Ontario. Although he wrote more extensively in English, he produced at least eight books fluently written in his mother tongue, some describing the work of the Highland bards, others discussing the lives and achievements of notable Gaels in the New World.

Elsewhere on this continent, the Gaelic language still appears in print, sometimes in quite unlikely places; for instance, in Oakland, California, a small bi-monthly magazine, *The Maple Leaf*, has devoted one of its pages to the language. But publishers, even when most patriotically Gaelic at heart, are no longer sufficiently enthusiastic to venture any outlay of money on such unprofitable business.

The following exchange of correspondence between Murdoch A. MacKenzie, the editor of a small Sydney paper, and one of his readers illustrates the problem.[44] A lady who signs herself "Bean Dhomhnuill" (Mrs. Donald) writes to him to complain:

> I buy the *Steelworker and Miner* every week, but lately I look in vain for the Gaelic songs which were wont to gladden my heart. What is the matter? Has your stock of Gaelic songs become exhausted? Or have the readers of Gaelic become luke-warm about their lovely language?

The editor answers:

> At the beginning of 1942 we began a Gaelic feature consisting mainly of classic Gaelic folk-songs. . . . We devoted a considerable portion of our available space and time to this feature up till a few months ago. . . .
>
> During all those months we have not received one word of encouragement, not one smile of commendation, not one token of appreciation, up till the time we received the above letter last week.
>
> We have been flooded with expressions of encouragement, commendation and appreciation, for our efforts in other directions. But as to our Gaelic feature—not even a distant rumble of response!
>
> It was purely a labour of love. Were we wasting sweetness on the desert air!
>
> To us Bean Dhomhnuill's letter above is as . . . an oasis to the thirsty traveller. We hereby thank her; and if we receive enough of similar requests to justify us in resuming the Gaelic feature, we shall be only too glad to resume it.

The publication which has remained the most consistently true to Gaelic is the newspaper that John Boyd established almost a century ago, the *Casket*. We have remarked that this paper was at first half English and half Gaelic and then gradually dropped the Gaelic section. In 1920 Father Donald M. MacAdam restored a Gaelic column in it once more;[45] later one of the professors at St. Francis Xavier University in Antigonish, Dr. (now Monsignor) Patrick J. Nicholson, took charge of editing the column. Monsignor Nicholson was born in Cape Breton and there acquired an extensive knowledge of Gaelic folk-culture and a keen ear for music. Trained as a scientist, he was put in charge of the physics department of the University but still retained his enthusiasm for the humanities; and, though busy with many teaching, administrative, and religious duties, he found time to contribute a column of Gaelic each week to the paper until he was promoted to the presidency of the University.

Monsignor Nicholson's work is of exceptional value and interest to the student of Gaelic lore. He gathered traditional songs and tales and recent compositions from a wide variety of informants. The material for his column was selected from this extensive collection, and though each weekly contribution was brief, over a period of more than twenty years the column accumulated many outstanding examples of Gaelic literature. Without it, the record of Gaelic publication in the New World would be less noteworthy.

7

Virtues and Vices

BESIDES their folk-culture, the Highland immigrants brought with them to the New World another intangible heritage—their religious faith. Like their secular culture it too played an important part in sustaining them during their first experiences in a strange country.

> Bho'n chuir gach cuis a bh' ann rium cul
> Dha'n d' thug mi run gu dian,
> 'S tim dhomh 'bhith na's tric' air m' urnuigh
> 'S leanachd dluth ri Dia.[1]

> Since every pursuit that once I turned my enthusiasm so keenly to has now been left behind me, it's time for me to pray more often and stand close to God.

So John the Hunter MacDonald, a Catholic bard who settled in Mabou, concludes his song of loneliness, composed on first arriving in Cape Breton.

The Highlander's heritage of faith and devotion to the church prospered, on the whole, in the New World, although it may be said to have flourished in the manner of a tree that unaccountably bears on the same branch both good fruit and bad.

Generalizations about the religion of the emigrants from the Highlands and Islands of Scotland are subject to many individual modifications, but it is safe to say that, at the period of the emigrations, the Catholic church had not sufficiently recovered from the disorganization produced by the Reformation and the subsequent defeat of the Stuart cause in the Rising of 1745 to minister adequately to all her Highland believers, nor had the Protestant churches of Scotland everywhere instructed the Highland adherents of the Reformed faith thoroughly in the religion which they professed. And when the settlers, both Catholic and Protestant, first arrived in North America, they had few opportunities to profit from the guidance and comfort of the clergy, who, for the most part, did not follow out after their flocks until some years had passed. Whenever they did accompany settlers to the New World, they were highly appreciated. Ann Gillis, one of a group of Catholics who ventured out to Glengarry County in 1802, composed a song on the advantages of the new environment in Upper Canada, and almost a third of it is devoted to praise and appreciation of Father Alexander Macdonell who escorted the emigrants:

> Bu mhath dhuinne 's gach doigh
> Maighstir Alasdair og,
> Fear na misnich, na treoir', 's na leirsinn,
>
> Dh'fhalbh e leinn, mar rinn Maois,
> Mach a duthaich na daors'
> 'Thoirt dhuinn fearainn, us saors', us eibhnis.[2]

Good to us in every way was Father Alexander Og, a man of courage, of vigour, of vision. He came with us, as Moses did, away from a country of want, to win land, prosperity, and happiness for us.

Tradition, in this case, tells us more than the song itself about the important part that the priest played in the lives of the pioneers. When Ann first arrived from Scotland, she was perpetually longing to be back in her old home, but Father Alexander said to her one day, " 'Anna bhochd, leig seachad a bhith caoidh na seann duthcha. Seo fhein duthaich a's fhearr dhuinne." (Poor Ann, stop lamenting for the old country. This country here is the best for us.) Thus rebuked she abandoned her nostalgia, accepted her lot in the New World, and composed the song from which the above quotation is excerpted.[3]

When the clergy first came out to the New World, their territory was so tremendous and the difficulties of travelling so desperate that they could reach only a small part of the people desiring their ministrations. The first Protestant Gaelic-speaking minister to arrive in Nova Scotia, for instance, the Reverend James MacGregor, came out from Scotland in 1786 and settled in Pictou County. There was already at that time an Episcopal church in Sydney, built for the military garrison, but no Presbyterian church or minister of any kind in the whole island of Cape

Breton. Since the island rapidly became crowded with Presbyterian Highlanders, who understood only Gaelic, the zealous young MacGregor longed to visit them. On one occasion he made a journey of more than 170 miles by horse and boat from Pictou to Sydney, to visit a Presbyterian family living there. We can imagine the time it took him to cover this distance.[4]

The few clergymen who came to Canada from Scotland in the first part of the nineteenth century were quite insufficient to cope with the great population they had to serve. Sectarian differences had to be forgotten. When they could reach no minister, Presbyterians had their children baptized by itinerant Catholic priests. And even in the later part of the century many communities were still supplied only irregularly. In the large Presbyterian community around Whycocomagh in Cape Breton, from the first arrival of a minister in 1837 until the end of the century, a period of sixty-three years, there were twenty-four years in which the pulpit was vacant. When the Reverend Peter MacLean, the first minister of the parish, returned on a visit in 1866 after a long absence in Scotland, he found over a hundred children waiting to be baptized. He performed the ceremony for them all at one gathering, which is still remembered as *am Baisteadh Mor* (the Great Baptism).[5] In other parts of the island there are those who can remember a time when mothers carried children for twenty and thirty miles to be baptized, and young couples travelled by horse or on foot or by row-boat for fifty miles and more in order to be joined in marriage.

The Catholic settlers were somewhat more fortunate in securing priests. To cite one example, shortly after the first Barra men settled around the Bras d'Or Lakes in Cape Breton, they were visited by a French bishop from Quebec; as early as 1820 a permanent priest was appointed, and from that time on there has been no interruption of the pastorate in that particular part of Cape Breton.[6] But many Catholic settlements were inadequately supplied at first; and churches were far apart. A Presbyterian Cape Bretoner who spent his youth at Gabarus recollects the difficulties of his Catholic neighbours: "I remember the MacIsaacs who used to live near us. They were Catholics. We used to see them early every Sunday morning walking past our house on their way to Mass. They were fasting, of course, and they had at least twelve miles to go. On the way back, we were the first house they would come to, and they'd always stop in for a visit and something warm to eat."

Religion was a potent force among the settlers, however difficult may have been the task of organizing churches among them. When they had no clergyman to aid them, Catholics and Protestants alike kept their faith alive by their own endeavours. The Catholics continued their custom of family prayers; the Protestants, their custom of family worship. Presbyterian settlers brought with them in their minds short pieces of exhortation, spiritual advice, and biblical interpretation which they had heard from ministers and catechists in Scotland and had treasured up in their hearts. These "notes," as they called them, they could recite from memory whenever a conversation called for spiritual edification.[7] Both Catholics and Protestants knew, however, that their religion would not survive without spiritual leaders, and they looked forward to the day when such men would come. They built churches in advance, hoping that a minister or a priest would some day arrive to take charge of the parish.

When once the clergy became established in the New World and began their work among the settlers, religion became an everyday topic of conversation and discussion. It pervaded the Highlander's daily life and actions. It was felt as an immediate and personal force always at work on every individual. The many Gaelic hymns composed in the New World present a clear picture of this feeling. Archibald MacDonald, the son of Presbyterian parents who settled in New Boston, Cape Breton,[8] composed a song on the death of his wife, and in it he recollects how she aided him in resisting evil:

> Bha suil aire aic' orm do ghnath,
> Mu'n tiginn air dleasdnas gearr,
> 'Gam chumail daonnan air mo gheard
> Mu'n cuireadh Satan smal orm.[9]

She always had a watchful eye on me lest I should swerve from duty, keeping me always on my guard before Satan could place his stain on me.

Nearly every Presbyterian family had a Gaelic Bible, and illiterate though the majority might be, there was always someone in the group who could read it to the rest. The Reverend Norman MacLeod of the Barony tells how he visited a poor Highlander in Pictou County during a visit to Canada in 1845.[10] The settler had emigrated from Mull at the age of five, was married, and lived with his family of six children in a small log cabin. He was poor and had suffered misfortune; he had lost a cow, and then a horse, and then a child. " 'But,' he said, handing me a large New Testament, 'that has been my sole comfort.' I was struck on opening it to find it a gift from 'the Duke of Sutherland to his friends and clansmen in America.' . . . The tears which streamed down that poor man's face while he pointed to that fine large printed Testament would be a great reward to the Duke for his gift, had he only witnessed them as I did."

No theologian could excel the regularity with which the Protestant Highlanders read the Bible or the thoroughness with which they studied its contents; no liturgist could recite the prayers of the Mass and the various forms of worship more correctly and fluently than the Catholic Highlanders. And both groups diligently studied the principles of their respective forms of Christian faith.

As the years went by, the missionary directors in Scotland saw to it that their Highland brethren across the seas were supplied with religious reading matter in their native tongue. The sermon-writers Doddridge, Baxter, and McCheyne were evidently favourites, but above them all stood John Bunyan. All the world knows Bunyan's *Pilgrim's Progress*, but few English readers today could pass an examination on the array of his works familiar to the Highlanders in Gaelic translation. A well-read student might know *Grace Abounding* and *The Holy War*, but how adequately would he deal with *Come and Welcome*, or *The World to Come*, or *Visions from Hell*, or *The Water of Life*, or *The Heavenly Footman*, or *Sighs from Hell*? Even today worn copies of these cherished treatises[11] may be found in the New World farm-houses; on a peaceful Sabbath day a white-haired and stooped old woman will still reread her beloved volume of Doddridge or Baxter, a smile of satisfaction lighting her lined

features as she murmurs to herself the familiar cadences of the
Gaelic translation.

Protestant Gaels were well supplied also with spiritual food
by the religious tracts that were distributed to them in profusion
by the Tract Societies of Edinburgh and Glasgow. To judge from
the stained and tattered condition of the still remaining copies,
their fragile leaves found eager readers.

The Catholic settler was likewise provided for. Families acquired Gaelic missals and catechisms and prayer books. As has
been mentioned, Father Ronald Rankin's *Gaelic Manual* was
republished in Charlottetown, Prince Edward Island, as early
as 1841 for the sake of Catholic Gaels who had settled in the
new land.

As an inseparable part of their worship both the Catholic and
the Protestant Gaels brought with them their own distinctive
church music. The Catholic clergy in Scotland, and those who
ministered to the settlers in the early years in the New World,
had usually been educated in Valladolid College in Spain, where
they learned the Gregorian music of their church. This they later
taught to their own Highland parishioners.

The church music and the method of singing brought to the
New World by the Presbyterian Gaels, on the other hand, were
both peculiarly products of the Scottish Reformation. Just as
the English-speaking branch of the Church of Scotland favoured
the use of metrical arrangements of the Psalms of David for
church worship, so did the Highlanders give a preference to
Gaelic metrical versions of the Psalms. After the Reformation,
Protestants discouraged the use of musical instruments in
churches; and congregations were therefore compelled to develop an ability for unaccompanied singing. Since printed hymn
books and psalm books were at first scarce and since many a
Highlander could not have read the words even if he did possess
a copy, a leader recited each stanza before the congregation sang
it. The subsequent development of Highland precented singing
is historically obscure,[12] but by the time of the emigrations this
much is clear: the precentor intoned each verse of the psalm,
one line at a time, in a sort of chant, which might be either
traditional or improvised; after the line had been precented, the

congregation sang it to a traditional tune, which did not necessarily bear any melodic relation to the precentor's chant. The tempo of the singing was slow, and stresses were marked by heavy crescendos. Unaccustomed listeners complain of a wailing tone, but musically trained judges are more likely to describe the effect as *maestoso*.

The settlers in their public worship perpetuated the custom. In the New World the precentor was highly respected by the community, and the precentor's box occupied a position in the church second in dignity only to the minister's pulpit. The settlers' descendants adhered to tradition so staunchly that it was not until late in the nineteenth century that they permitted in their churches the now familiar organ and English hymn book; and the records suggest that no congregation welcomed the innovation unanimously.[13]

The people sang religious music at home as well as in church, but within the home the hymns composed by Peter Grant of Strathspey were perhaps more popular than the elaborate precented psalms. In his *Dain Spioradail* (Spiritual Songs) Grant used simple language and colourful imagery, and he set his words to secular tunes popular in the Highlands. The hymns were first published in Scotland early in the nineteenth century and aroused such demand that new copies had to be issued repeatedly. In the New World, as we have seen, editions appeared within a ten-year interval (1826-36) in Fayetteville, North Carolina, and in Montreal, Lower Canada—somewhat of an international publishing record for a Gaelic writer. The settlers adapted Grant's hymns to the role of the traditional occupational songs: mothers sang them as lullabies to their children, housewives sang them while they spun yarn at the spinning-wheel, old women sang them on the barrens of Cape Breton while their younger companions gathered blueberries.

For the Presbyterians in the New World the most important religious event of the year was Communion Week, a ceremony imported from Scotland. Communion Week was celebrated wherever there was a Presbyterian church, or even where there was none. Men, women, and children gathered from far and near. Some walked twenty, forty, and even fifty miles; walked barefoot carrying a pair of shoes in their hands so that their foot-wear would be fresh for the occasion. They slept in the barns and farm-houses of their friends and were fed by them. House-wives in Cape Breton remember serving meals to as many as a hundred visiting celebrants every day during the five-day ceremony.

The celebration began on Thursday, when the people gathered to humiliate themselves before God. Friday was devoted to the *ceisd* (question)—a period of absorbing interest to all present. A worthy elder of the congregation presented a text before the gathering, and those who were skilled in theological subtleties —especially other elders of the church—were called upon to demonstrate, in the light of the text, the marks of a true Christian. Many who spoke were not widely read and possessed little formal education, but their knowledge of the Scriptures was profound, and they applied this knowledge in a manner which their descendants, although better schooled, claim they cannot equal. The underlying purpose of the discussion was that those who felt they had succeeded in the difficult task of living a Christian life should provide encouragement and advice to weaker mortals. Occasionally the self-righteous used the *ceisd* as an opportunity to enlarge on their own virtues by self-praise, and to defame their neighbours by pointed thrusts and invidious comparisons. But such offensive and unchristian tactics did not escape rebuke. On one occasion a respected lay catechist, Duncan MacDonald of Boulardrie, or Donnchadh Ban Ceisdear, to give him the Gaelic name by which he was known throughout Cape Breton, after listening to the long harangue of a malicious back-biter, rose and said, "Chan ann gu bhith tolladh nan uan a chuireadh adhaircean air na caoraich." (It is not for the purpose of goring the lambs that horns were put on the sheep.) He then proceeded to deliver his own gentle and kindly advice.[14]

Saturday was dedicated to the spiritual preparation of those who were to receive Communion on the following day. The sacrament on Sunday was the climax of the Communion Week. No church was large enough to contain the crowds which assembled, and the service was therefore conducted out of doors. A tent for the clergy was pitched in a large field near the church; the Communion table, covered with white linen, was set in front of the tent; and benches for the communicants were arranged in rows on the grass. Here, in the open air, more than a thousand people would congregate to celebrate the Lord's Supper in the traditional manner practised by their forefathers in the Highlands and Islands of Scotland. On Monday a final service of thanksgiving was held, after which the celebrants returned to their homes throughout the countryside.

Those who can still recall the solemn and worshipful spirit of Communion Week admit with a tolerant smile that, like the Holy Fair in the Lowlands of Scotland described by Burns, it was also the occasion for outbursts of youthful wildness which contrasted grotesquely with the piety of the older people. The Reverend James MacGregor complained bitterly about the frivolous attitude of the first congregations which gathered to hear him in Pictou County, and he speaks of being forced in Prince Edward Island to read the psalm at the top of his lungs in order to drown out the idle chatter of the inattentive worshippers.[15] He early succeeded in instilling into his congregations a more reverent spirit, but the frivolous tendency which he combatted survived in other Highland communities until much more recent times. People still living in Cape Breton remember how the girls and boys standing at the back of the crowd during an open-air service would throw sugar candy down on the sun shades of the people in front of them until, as one informant said, "You would think to hear the rattle on the umbrellas that you were sitting out in a heavy hail-storm." And this lack of reverence towards the spiritual was not characteristic of the very young only; unmarried men and women delighted in the opportunity that Communion Week afforded them to leave home and go a-courting; and those who relished liquor found ample to satisfy them on such occasions though nominally they had assembled for another purpose. Tradition tells of a minister in the past century who, in the course of conducting a communion service in the Mira district of Cape Breton, found a merchant hidden in the woods with a barrel of rum which he hoped to sell to those in attendance. The minister gained the awed respect of the people, although not perhaps their unqualified admiration, by overturning the rum onto the ground. But his drastic action does not seem to have eradicated the custom of selling liquor on such occasions, for we read that in 1901 in the same district a liquor seller was again found hiding with his supply near a church which was to celebrate communion; in this case, he was routed out and subsequently brought before a magistrate and fined $50.[16]

Ironically, the faults of the Highlander often seem to stem from his religion.[17] Church questions, for instance, which were always debated with considerable fervour and ingenuity, were perilously apt to end in bitterness and strife. The Disruption of the Church of Scotland in 1843 had the most pernicious effect on the Highland communities in the New World. John MacKay, Stipendiary Magistrate of New Glasgow, a Highlander who came out to Pictou County in 1805 at the age of eleven, speaks in his memoirs[18] of the distressing effects which he himself witnessed in his own country:

> About 1815 religious questions began to disturb the community, principally denominational questions. The original inhabitants were mainly from the Highlands of Scotland and belonged to the Established Church. Very little was known at that time here of sectarian distinctions which were then beginning to obtain from Scotland. Rev. Dr. MacGregor, the first minister of Pictou, belonged to the body then known there as Seceders; but, being a good man and an earnest preacher, no exception was taken to him on that account. Indeed, the distinction was scarcely intelligible to them.

The distiction which he mentions became by 1843 such a bitterly debated point of dissension that he writes of this period: "These were dark and gloomy days. We were bewildered. No man knew scarcely what to do, or whom to place confidence in or ask for advice. Old ties of friendship were broken up; the peace of families was destroyed; and strife and bad blood were rife far and near."

The Union of the various branches of the Presbyterian Church in Canada in 1875 likewise produced several thorny points of disagreement on matters of church government. These were well debated, but the final decision in many communities brought bloodshed with it and tragic family feuds which remained for long unassuaged. The question of the Union of the Presbyterian, Methodist, and Congregationalist churches in Canada in 1925 gave rise to many similar unchristian incidents.

Even ministers were carried away with the fury of debates over matters of principle; and it has been complained that their intolerant severity towards back-sliders in itself did not serve as a very edifying example of the Christian way of life. An eloquent Gaelic-speaking minister, born in Scotland, preached a farewell sermon to his Cape Breton congregation with such fire and passion that he found it necessary to break off in the midst of his exhortation until the weeping of his congregation had subsided. Yet tradition reports that, when a penurious farmer had been unable to pay his share of the stipend, this same eloquent minister had seized the debtor's only cow.

It is, of course, inevitable that people should remember the scandalous rancour of religious disputes and yet forget the progress achieved by those who believed in their views and considered it their duty to defend their cause. If dissension arose during the difficult process of seeking the truth, perhaps it was, after all, only a healthy sign. More serious perhaps was the frequent failure of religion to control the daily lives and morals of the settlers. They had hard and unforgiving tempers and were loath to overlook an insult or allow a feud to die out. They retained curious and unreasonable prejudices which their forefathers had once fostered in Scotland but which had no possible foundation in the new land.

The clannishness with which these prejudices were associated had its finer qualities but unfortunately encouraged stubborn pig-headedness. Mrs. MacDonald can quote an example of this spirit. She was born and reared in Big Baddeck, Cape Breton; most of her neighbours were MacLeods. Her mother and father, however, were both MacLeans by birth and came from the island of Muck. Now, the MacLeans of Muck disapproved of the Mac-Leods as a matter of principle. Therefore if Mrs. MacDonald, when a little girl at school, brought a young MacLeod home with her for a meal, the visitor would be fed without complaint, according to the laws of Highland hospitality; but afterward the MacLean parents would warn their daughter that she must never again bring a MacLeod to the house if she could possibly avoid it. Each clan had a rime about a rival clan, and a very offensive saying it might sometimes be. The MacLeods, for

instance, were evidently disliked by clans other than the Mac-
Lean, for one of the Ferguson clan living in Cape Breton remembers a rime of the type mentioned:

> MacLeoid na h-Earradh 's a thon air faileadh;
> MacAsgaill an garbhan na seann mine-corc.
>
> MacLeod of Harris, and the skin off his bottom;
> MacAskill, the leavings of the old oat-meal.

Just what gave rise to this rime, and at what pecularities of the
MacLeods and MacAskills it was scoffing, the informant did not
know. But it may be easily understood that to repeat such a
rime in the hearing of a sensitive member of either clan would
be a sure invitation to a fight.

Clan animosities entered even into the music of the Highlanders. Practised in the art of impromptu riming, they could quickly
compose satirical stanzas to accompany a popular tune. Much
to the irritation of their victims these new words were very apt
to become as popular as the tune itself. So scathing was
the invective of the verses set to the air known as "Roy's Wife"
or "An Caimbeulach Dubh" (The Black Campbell) that no
loyal Campbell ever after cared to hear the tune even when
devoid of its refrain. An unknown satirist composed some very
uncomplimentary verses about the Rankins to fit the old tune,
"Piuthar Mhic-a-Phi" (MacPhee's Sister); the satire was so
effective that the tune was renamed "Am Port Chloinn'-'ic-
Raing" (The Rankins' Tune), and so offensive that the mere
sound of the music could produce pandemonium at any gathering in Mabou, Cape Breton, a stronghold of the Rankins. And
in the Margaree district, where the MacDougalls are very
numerous, it was highly inadvisable to play the tune known by
the innocent title, "Am Muileann Dubh" (The Black Mill), for a
reason even more curious. One line of a stanza set to this tune
runs: "Tha nead na circe fraoiche 's a' mhuileann dubh" (In the
black mill is the heather-hen's nest); and the MacDougalls of
Margaree, because of some joke about hens once told at the
expense of their clan, were so sensitive that they could not
tolerate a reference to poultry of any kind and were likely to
regard even the playing of the tune as a veiled insult.

Of all the bitternesses between clans, that between the Mac-
Donalds and the Campbells was the most pronounced. It is
popularly supposed that the massacre of the MacDonalds of
Glencoe in 1692 was the cause, but actually the rivalry of the
two clans resulted from the working of complex political causes
over a long span of years. The MacDonalds were the most
powerful of all the clans in the days of clan independence; at
the same time they were the most remote from Edinburgh, the
centre where a unified governmental control of Scotland was
destined to become established. The territory of the Campbells,
on the other hand, lay near to Edinburgh, and the Campbell
leaders astutely championed the cause of this central power
whenever possible.[19] In this way, presumably not unintentionally, they increased their own influence. In carrying out re-
tributive measures on behalf of the central government, they
frequently had occasion to exert force against rebellious clans,
and against none more frequently than the powerful Mac-
Donalds. The resulting enmity between the two clans persisted
among the settlers, although power-politics no longer played
any part.

Illustrations of this rivalry in the New World may readily be
found. When the Gaelic newspaper *Mac-Talla* in 1898 published
a short history of the Campbells, one reader, a MacDonald, was
not at all satisfied. In a letter to the editor[20] he indignantly
pointed out that the account presented only the fine side of the
picture and ignored the rough:

> Thog na Caimbeulaich iad fein le cealgaireachd us mealltaireachd,
> agus le bhith cur ceap-tuislidh roimh chinnidheann saor-chridheach
> eile, mar a bha na Domhnullaich, na Leathainich agus na Griogairich.

> The Campbells raised themselves by trickery and deception, and by
> setting stumbling blocks before other, free-hearted clans, such as
> the MacDonalds, the MacLeans, and the MacGregors.

He concluded his letter by quoting passages from the works of
four Highland bards in support of his view. While sober history
reveals that every clan had both faults and virtues, this letter
shows how unwilling the members of one clan were to forget the
faults of a rival, no matter what his fine qualities might be.

The traditional rivalries were not, however, always taken so
seriously in the New World, even those as age-old and intense
as that between the MacDonalds and the Campbells, and seem
to have abated gradually during the nineteenth century. A
MacDonald woman, from Prince Edward Island, now advanced
in years, remembers that as a child she all unwittingly pinned up
on the wall a picture of the Duke of Argyll. Her MacDonald
father noticed the picture, and when he recognized in amazed
horror that the features were those of the chief of the hated rival
clan, Clan Campbell, he immediately ordered her to destroy it
in the fire. But in telling her story she adds with a quiet smile,
"But it was a Campbell that my father married when he wanted
a wife, just the same."

In a crisis, moreover, the Gaels have proved that they are
capable of uniting in a common front against a national enemy;
and on such occasions even the bards are willing to submerge
the individualities of the clan in a general encomium of the
whole race. Note, for example, the *Song of the Gaels*[21] composed
by John the Piper MacGillivray, who served as a clan bard
before emigrating to Antigonish:

> 'S iad na Gaidheil fein na gaisgich,
> Na suinn chruadha, chuanta, sgairteil.
> Bhiodh an t-eileadh grinn 's an gartan
> Anns gach baiteal bhuadhach.
>
> Nuair dh' eireadh meanmna 'n an spiorad
> Bhiodh na garbh-bhuillich gun ghiorag
> (Mar choin gharg an sealg a' millidh)
> Ann am mire an fhuathais.
>
> Cha robh streup 's an robh chuid armailt
> Eadar an Eiphit us a' Ghearmailt
> Nach robh Iodhainn treun na h-Albann
> Le'n cuid clag 'g a bhualadh.
>
> Nise chan eil cearn 's an t-saoghal
> 'S nach eil meas orra mar dhaoine.
> 'S balla laidir do'n luchd-gaoil iad
> 'S aognaicht' le'n luchd-fuath iad.

It's the Highlanders who are heroes, hardy, handsome, manly
warriors. The magnificent kilt and bonnet in every battle were
victorious.

When passion was aroused in their spirits, the hard-strikers were
dauntless (like a savage hound in hunt for slaughter) in the uproar
of horror.

There was never a combat where an army was engaged from Egypt
to Germany without a brave band from Scotland wielding their
weapons.

Now there's no part of the world where they aren't respected for
their manhood. They're a strong protection to their friends and
terrifying to their enemies.

It is difficult to imagine to what heights his eulogies might have
soared if he had lived to witness the performance of Canadian
Highland regiments during the First and Second World Wars.

Prejudices must nevertheless have been detrimental to the
welfare of the first Highland settlements, particularly among
those settlers who were prone to intemperance. There can be
no doubt that the Scots' notorious fondness for whisky produced
untold harm among the more unruly. The Reverend James Mac-
Gregor did not disapprove of taking a warming glass himself,
but he was horrified at the excesses to which his charges in the
New World allowed themselves to go. He wrote in 1809, "Once
in a day I could not have believed that all the vices in the world
would have done so much damage in Pictou as I have seen
drunkenness alone do within these few years."[22] Home-made
whisky and, later, the rival American drink, rum, were as
plentiful as water in the pioneering settlements, and although
the temperance movement and strict liquor laws subsequently
did much to improve conditions, liquor continued to be a
stumbling-block for many of the settlers' descendants.

Probably the majority of the people did not overindulge in
its use, and it is true, liquor promoted joviality at their gatherings, but it often led to more than that. It resulted in the
squandering of money, the neglect of promising farms, the
break-up of families; it caused endless quarrels and, on occasions,
savage bloodshed. It was a dangerous stimulant among people
who cultivated such intense prejudices and rivalries. For that
reason the happiest and most innocent occasions might lead
to disaster. Any gathering, particularly a milling frolic or a
wedding, was considered to be a reasonable excuse for a dance,

and a dance always called for liquor. As a consequence rural dances became traditionally associated with fights. Under the exciting influence of a lively fiddle and dancing feet, and the hazardous inspiration of rum and whisky, petty feuds burst into flame, bravado flourished, and some blood-thirsty youth would leap at his rival. Usually all that resulted from the fight was a few bruises and a cut or two, but sometimes such a fight did not end until one of the participants had been killed. Late in the last century in one of the Highland communities in Cape Breton two rivals went to a ploughing frolic. After the ploughing was completed and the dancing had warmed up, Alec, one of the rivals, attacked John, the other. When it seemed that Alec was not likely to win the fight, Alec's brother, Hector, at the instigation of his father, joined in. John was then at a great disadvantage, but his brother Peter in turn came to his aid. Peter was a cripple and therefore not particularly powerful. When Hector began to worst him, in the fury of the fight he drew a knife, and stabbed at his opponent, and killed him.[23] That the outcome of this trivial feud is not typical, however, is proved by the fact that the present members of the community still speak of it in tones of horror.

Even funerals were enlivened by a liberal indulgence in hard liquor. Judge John G. Marshall, who knew the Cape Breton of the early nineteenth century and its people well, tells how the funeral of a Highland woman about the year 1836 led to a whole series of court cases.[24] Since it had been the wish of the deceased to be buried in her parents' grave-lot, a party of her Highland neighbours undertook to carry her remains on the journey, a distance of some forty miles. They fortified themselves well before setting out, and to learn of the outcome we may best turn to the Judge's account, which unintentionally heightens the drollery of the situation by its incongruously legalistic and pompous style:

> . . . either from some immediate provocation or old clan or family strife or bad feeling a quarrel while on the way arose between the two parties, which being intensified or rendered more violent by the action of the strong liquor on their own naturally ardent passions, from words they proceeded to blows and for a part of a day kept up a

kind of running battle along the road, during which they battered and bruised each other most severely. At the ensuing term of the court in that county a number of what may be called cross or opposite indictments were found against several of the combattants belonging to each party, and a considerable portion of the term was taken up in trying those cases.

It would be historically unsound, however, to seize on these examples of animal spirits as a proof that the Highlander's religion was only a farce or that the many devout people who paid it service were hypocrites—charges which the cynical agnosticism of the early twentieth century used to level against the piety of the nineteenth century. The dramatic exceptions readily blind us to the good which religion accomplished. We may conceive of the work of the church in the New World as a great force driving all before it. As the result of its impetus some veered to the extreme of fanaticism and others to the extreme of revulsion, but the majority moved ahead on the paths of moderation.

An old Gaelic proverb tells us, "Is iomadh duine laghach a mhill an creideamh." (There's many a delightful person that has been spoiled by religion.) Probably the saying refers to the two extreme cases: to the rebel, on the one hand, who refuses to accept any moral guidance, and to the fanatic, on the other, who appears in many guises—the ascetic parent who renounces worldly joy and autocratically forces the same doctrine on his children, the Pharisee who carps at his neighbours, or the dogmatist who fights over minute differences of doctrine and forgets the main principles. But between these two extremes are the many Highland settlers and their descendants who humbly tried to imitate the way of Christ.

8

~~~~~~

Improvements

THE FIRST Highland settlers in the New World could still remember the days when the chieftains of the clans had provided their followers with paternal guidance; the more recent emigrants had been subject to the control and authority of a landlord. All settlers were therefore conscious of having won a new freedom from the restrictions once imposed upon them by their superiors; but the change was not entirely a gain, for now they lacked the leaders who could guide them in their use of this unaccustomed liberty.[1] To cultivate their fields and stock their farms intelligently; to catch the teeming fish efficiently; to market their produce profitably; to educate their children; to establish churches in their settlements; to co-operate with their neighbours; to share in the government of their new land—these were problems which the Highland settlers were often ill prepared to face.

Some of the settlers did not concern themselves greatly with the problems of adaptation and self-improvement. After undergoing the strain of parting from Scotland and surviving the first difficult years in the New World, they were content to relax from any further effort beyond the minimum required to secure food and clothing for themselves and their families. Those who did not understand the background of these Highland settlers gave them a poor character.

A traveller who visited a Highland settlement in Glengarry County, Ontario, about the year 1819 was disappointed by the lack of progress shown by the settlers. He admitted that they had been poorly provided when they arrived and that they faced the difficulties of a strange climate, an inaccessible location, inadequate roads, and the discouraging uncertainty of the forests.

Yet he complained that the people seemed to be "unambitious" and showed "no inclination to improve their mode of life." Many were still living in nothing better than a one-roomed log cabin.[2] The Reverend Thomas Trotter similarly complained in 1820 that the Highlanders of the Antigonish district were "ignorant and lazy"; he had been trying to organize an effective agricultural society in the district and met with the most discouraging lack of support.[3] Actually, many of the Highlanders could not understand the English language sufficiently well to comprehend Mr. Trotter's advice, and even those who could were not particularly prone to speculate about improvement and reform. New methods of agriculture when they had enough to eat, and the saving of labour when their families included an abundance of able-bodied helpers, were matters of small concern to them.

Captain Moorsom, travelling in 1830 through the Highland settlement around St. Mary's River in Guysborough County, noticed the same quality among the Highlanders there which had offended Mr. Trotter's managerial instincts, but he understood better the underlying reason for this apparent indifference. These settlers, he explains, "make but indifferent farmers; accustomed to a hard and penurious mode of life, they are too easily satisfied with the bare existence that even indolence can procure in this country, and care little for raising themselves and their families to a state of comfort and abundance."[4]

Similarly, as another commentator points out, the Skye settlers in Prince Edward Island were satisfied with the simplest and roughest type of house and did not try to improve the appearance of their property, until the surrounding English homes, with their trim exteriors and neat hedges, influenced the Highlanders to imitate the more refined ways of their neighbours.[5]

The Highlanders were not, in fact, lazy. Their previous environment had encouraged an attitude towards life that demanded only a very meagre standard of living so long as there was ample opportunity for amusement and happiness. The Highlander was thus more of an artist than a labourer, and it is through the utterances and actions of the artists that we can best understand his philosophy of life. When John the Piper MacGillivray,[6] who

had been family piper to the laird of Glenaladale, was reduced
to the simple farming and fishing life of the New World, he
indignantly insisted that his role in life was still to provide music
and not to toil. The Bard MacLean rejoiced in the day when his
children grew to the age that they were able to tend the farm
without requiring the unenthusiastic assistance of their poet-
father.[7] Angus Campbell complained that in the New World,
unlike Scotland, no patron bestows timely gifts on the poet to
spare him from the dull round of daily toil.[8] Murdoch Morrison
epitomizes the attitude of the Highland artist in a homely phrase
when he quotes the reproach which his daughter levels at him:

> Tha sibh math gu leor dheth;
> Chan eil aon char agaibh ach smokeadh us orain.[9]

> You're well enough off; the only concern you have is for smoking
> and songs.

There was something of the artist's zest for songs and music and
leisure in every Highland settler, and even if the happy-go-lucky
philosophy may have produced some slovens, yet it also produced those well-rounded and genial spirits who refused to
become so entirely immersed in the everyday cares of the world
as to forget the graces of life.

Whatever may have been the charm of the Highlander's
character, however, he could not co-operate very happily with
the English-speaking settlers in the New World until he had
learned to read and speak the English language and had mastered
the conventional outlines of formal education. The task of
arousing him to this necessity was at first difficult. The Reverend
James MacGregor, who attacked the problem in Pictou County
with vigour, wrote in 1826, as he looked back over his educational efforts: "Many of the Highlanders were perfectly indifferent
about education, for neither themselves nor any of their ancestors had ever tasted its pleasure or its profit."[10] In a song of his
own composition he enlarges on the serious effects of their
ignorance:

> Bha na Gaidheil ro aineolach, dhall,
> Bha ionnsachadh gann 'n am measg:
> Bha 'n eolas cho tana, 's cho mall,
> 'S nach b' aithne dhoibh 'n call a mheas.

Cha chreideadh iad buannachd no stath
'Bhith 'n sgoileireachd ard d' an cloinn,
Ged fheudadh iad 'fhaicinn gach la
Gur i thog o'n lar na Goill.

Ach b' annsa leo 'n airgid 's an oir
A chaitheadh gu gorach truagh
Ri amaideachd, oranaibh, 's ol,
Ri bainnsibh 's ri ceol d' an cluais.
Chan iongnadh ged bha iad gun chail
Do fhacal na slaint aig Dia,
Ged choisinn an namhaid an gradh,
'S ged bha iad toirt da a mhiann.[11]

The Gaels were very ignorant and blind; learning was scarce among them. Their instruction was so shallow and slow that they didn't recognize the measure of their loss. They wouldn't believe that there was any profit or gain in formal schooling for their children, although they could see every day that it was this which had raised the English-speaking people from the ground.

They preferred to spend their silver and gold stupidly and sordidly on folly, songs, and drink, on weddings, and on music for their ears. No wonder that they had no appetite for God's word of salvation, that the Enemy won their affection, and that they allowed him his will!

Gradually his efforts and the efforts of other public-spirited educators began to show their effect. MacGregor admitted he found it easier than he had thought "to rouse the Highlanders to attend to the education of their children, so far as to read the Bible."[12] As his endeavours prospered he was moved to predict a great future for the people he strove so hard to serve:

Ach theid aineolas nis as an tir
'S gach cleachdadh neo-dhireach, crom,
Us mealaidh sinn sonas us sith
Gun fharmad no stri 'n ar fonn.
Theid sgoilean chur suas anns gach cearn;
Bidh leabhraichean Gaidhlig pailt;
Bidh eolas us diadhachd ag fas;
Thig gach duine gu stath 's gu rath.

Nis togaidh na Gaidheil an ceann,
'S cha bhi iad am fang na's mo;
Bidh aca ard fhoghlum nan Gall
Us tuigse neo-mhall 'n a choir.

Theid innleachdan 's oibrean air bonn
'Chuireas saibhreas 'n ar fonn gu pailt.
Bidh 'n diblidh cho laidir ri sonn,
'S am bochd cha bhi lom le h-airc.[13]

Ignorance will now pass away from the land and every unrighteous and corrupt custom, and we shall enjoy happiness and peace without envy or strife in our country. Schools will be built in every quarter; Gaelic books will be plentiful; knowledge and godliness will grow; every man will become useful and productive.

Now the Gaels will raise their heads, and they will be in bondage no longer. They will have the formal education of the English-speaking people and ready intelligence along with it. Plans and operations will be established which will spread wealth plentifully through our country. The weak will be as strong as the warrior, and the poor no longer be enfeebled by want.

Education could scarcely effect in any society a transformation as Utopian as the poet envisioned, but education did awaken a remarkable response. When once the Gaels in the rural settlements became literate, the alert-minded and ambitious young children among them were fired with a desire to obtain further education. They acquired at their local schools a sound foundation of learning and carried away with them the will to succeed; they saved money and went to college. Many of them entered the professions. The Highland settlements now proudly boast that they have sent native sons forth over the whole continent as ministers, priests, doctors, lawyers, judges, politicians, and professors.

At one time in St. Louis, Missouri, three ministers—a MacLeod, a Matheson, and a MacIvor—held important charges, each in one of the large city churches. All three of them were born in Little Narrows, Cape Breton—a Highland settlement—and as children were educated in various neighbouring country school houses.

For the production of professional men the district of Lake Ainslie is generally recognized as the outstanding rural section within Cape Breton, and many examples of the country boy winning a place of respect in the professions might be quoted in substantiation of its claim. The most striking is offered by the family of John MacKinnon of Kirkwood, on the east side of the lake. He married a Catherine MacLean, and they reared nine sons on their farm. Five of these sons—Alexander D., Murdoch A., Hector L., Archibald D., and John Y.—went through college and became ministers. Another son—Neil—died while preparing for the ministry. Two of the sons—Donald L. and Hugh—went through college and became doctors. The ninth—Malcolm D.—remained on the farm to take over its management when his father died.

But we do not need to limit our survey to Cape Breton. Everywhere we find the settlers' children profiting from education. The family of Allan Cameron in Pomquet, Antigonish County, consisted of eleven boys and six girls. Of the girls three became nuns; two married but had no children; and one married and became the mother of two nuns and a lawyer. Three of the boys became priests. One became a doctor. Of the remaining seven boys, one raised a family in which there was one nun; one raised a family in which there were two nuns and two lawyers; and one raised a family in which there were four nuns.

Thus the record of distinction has been upheld by the generations born of the original Highland emigrants, wherever they have settled in the New World. By searching through the various *Who's Who* publications one could compile an impressive list of men and women who were born and raised in these rural communities. The advocates of education proved their contention, and the children to whom this education was offered proved themselves worthy of the educators' care.

There is something rather remarkable, on first thought, about the prominence which so many of the people of Highland stock attained in the New World. Who would have imagined that the people who were reduced virtually to a peasant existence in Scotland after the defeat of 1746 would produce such an abundance of professional men and leaders after emigration to the New World? But we must not be deceived by the false implications of the term "peasant." The Highland way of life was primitive as the result of an unhappy history and a difficult environment, but the mentality of the Highlander, peasant though we call him, did not correspond in any way to the level which we unreflectingly associate with that status. In fact, Norman MacLeod of the Barony assures us that, after compar-

ing the Highland peasantry with that of many countries, he is
convinced that his countrymen are "by far the most intelligent
in the world."[14] If he—himself a Highlander—were the only one
to make this claim, his testimony might very well be considered
prejudiced, but various travellers,[15] writing dispassionately, convey the same impression when they describe the personal dignity,
gentlemanliness, and mental alertness possessed by even the
most destitute inhabitants of the Highlands and Islands.

There is, then, no real paradox in the fact that the son of the
Highland bard becomes in the New World a distinguished judge,
and the son of a fiddler an eloquent minister. The genius of the
people is only finding new channels of expression. In Scotland
the latent ability of the Highlander had enjoyed little opportunity for development. His creative energy was spent on the
ephemeral pursuits of his folk-culture, on dancing and singing
and composing songs. He gave the impression of being indifferent
and unambitious in material matters, but, as Norman MacLeod
reminds us,

> the circumstances of his country, his small "croft" and want of
> capital, the bad land and hard weather, with the small returns for his
> uncertain labour, have tended to depress rather than to stimulate him.
> . . . when he is removed to another clime, and placed in more favour-
> able circumstances, he exhibits a perseverance and industry which
> make him rise very rapidly.[16]

Moreover, while history may have denied the settlers material
prosperity, their dying clan system had bequeathed to them, as
almost its only legacy, a deeply rooted belief in the rights and
worth of the individual, which played an important part in
forming the character of their descendants. "Why did the people
from Lake Ainslie do so well as doctors and lawyers and ministers? Well, I can tell you," says an old Cape Bretoner. "They
weren't afraid of anything or anybody. When they went to
school they said to themselves that if other people could master
the learning necessary for a doctor or a lawyer or a minister, so
could they. Then they worked hard and accomplished whatever
they set their mind to."

The remote and isolated positions in which the pioneers settled
may, curiously enough, also have played an important part in

shaping the character of their offspring. When once the first unsettled pioneering days had passed, the discipline of the church, of the school, and of the family became firmly established. In the simple country life of the people these powerful influences were not impeded by the distractions now so familiar to those who live in wealthy urban centres. A well-informed minister, writing in 1921 on the history of the Presbyterian church in Cape Breton,[17] remarks that the churches in the island have been supplied almost exclusively with ministers who were reared in rural districts. His explanation for the failure of the urban communities reminds us of the potentialities of the country as a training ground for the formation of intellect, imagination, and spirituality: "Industrial centres are not good breeding grounds for preachers of any denomination. There is a large demand for labour at good pay, and the boys yield to the ever-present temptation to become wage-earners rather than students. Indeed, it is difficult to keep them in the common school long enough to be more than half prepared for the duties of life." Whenever a poor country boy makes good, we are quick to praise the manner in which he has overcome his disadvantages, and yet his very poverty and rural background may well have been the guides which led him to the path of success.

Between the period of their settlement and the present day the way of life of the country people has been affected not merely by new educational opportunities but also by a revolutionary economic change. The old-timers in the Canadian Maritimes jokingly sum up this process in an often-quoted aphorism: "When I was a boy, I was brought up on porridge and the Bible. But now, all I see is corn-flakes and Eaton's catalogue." The observation, like many another folk-saying, is penetrating.

The country life which the settlers knew only a few generations ago was a primitive existence: they raised their own food and made their own clothing, furniture, and housing. Now the farmer or the fisherman is almost entirely urbanized; he buys from the city, he sells to the city, he specializes in some particular type of farming or fishing as a business and makes his income from that. His way of life now differs but little from that of the city business man except that his occupation is out of doors rather than in an office.

True to the implications of the folk-saying, the wife serves her husband with corn-flakes for breakfast; ready-made cereal saves her the trouble of cooking. What she needs for the house she orders from the mail-order catalogue. The machine age has replaced handiwork. And, if we believe the folk-saying in its entirety, the new materialism even threatens to displace the Christian religion.

This alteration, which has by now affected almost the entire world, is so well recognized that it may scarcely appear to merit further discussion, but the effects of the change on the Highland settlers are of particular interest. No immigrants were as a group more completely peasant in their way of life when first they arrived on these shores than the men and women who came from the remote valleys and sea-coasts of the Highlands and Islands of Scotland. The process of change has been slow, gradual, and imperceptible, but the effects have been overwhelming.

Communications between settlements began to improve. Roads were built through the forests; rivers and inlets were bridged. Isolated settlers were no longer obliged to row with their produce to the nearest landing point and carry it on their backs from there to the market, and to bring home their supplies and seed by foot. The difference that the automobile has made in modern life is as nothing compared to the difference that good roads and bridges and swift horses, or even sturdy oxen, made in the life of the pioneer settlers of the New World.

Trade developed. Ships found a market for the products of the country and imported new luxuries from the outside world to the pioneers. Market towns developed. The farmer no longer planted, sowed, reaped, cultivated, and bred stock for the subsistence of his household only; he raised produce to sell. The fisherman was no longer satisfied with catching enough to feed his family; he began to deal in fish by the barrelful rather than the potful; he sold for cash.

In combination with this change in the way of life came the wonders of the mechanical age. Labour-saving devices, once undreamed of, were introduced to the country people. No one unfamiliar with country life can appreciate the extent to which these innovations liberated the farmer and fisherman from drudgery and toil. Vincent MacLellan, in a song published at the end of the nineteenth century, explains the benefits of the mowing machine and the horse-drawn rake:

> Mar tha an saoghal tighinn air adhart
> 'S mor a' chobhair do chlann daoine;
> Chan eil iad fo shaothair le obair,
> Roimh 'n am a chromas le aois iad.
> 'S mor an t-saoirsinneachd dha 'm bodhaig
> Bho'n a gheibh iad tighinn as aonais,
> 'S gach ionnsramaid 'tha air tighinn am follais
> Ni 'n diugh dhaibh obair nan daoine.
>
> Chan eil obair ri a dheanamh
> Air fiar ann mar bha e aon uair.
> Chan fhaicear duine le speal gheur
> 'G a ghearradh sios le neart a ghaoirdean,
> Ach uidheam rothach le cogs iaruinn,
> Le eich shrianaich us fear 'g an stiuradh,
> Us e mar shabh ann le 'chuid fhiaclan
> A ghearras sios gach dias gun saothair.
>
> Cha mho a chithear baidean nigheanag
> A' falbh le sgrioban 'n an glacaibh,
> Le curam mor us le mor-dhichioll
> Gu finid 'chur air an achadh.
> 'S ann chithear gille og a' direadh
> Air innleachd, us each 'g a tharruing,
> A thruiseas suas am fiar 'n a mhill
> Cho luath ri stuadh a' direadh cladaich.[18]

As the world is progressing the children of men are finding great relief; they are not enslaved by work which stoops them with old age before their time. There is a great liberation for their bodies since they have been able to escape from it, and every machine which has been invented today performs the work of human beings for them.

There's no work to be done on the hay now such as there used to be at one time. No longer do you see a man with a sharp scythe cutting it down by the exertion of his arms, but a device equipped with wheels and iron cogs, with bridled horses and a man steering them; it is like a saw with its set of teeth cutting down each blade without effort.

No longer will you see a group of young girls going out with rakes in their hands, busily and diligently tidying off the field. Now you see a young boy climbing up on a horse-drawn machine which gathers up the hay in piles as quickly as a wave races up the shore.

We might not suspect that contrivances apparently so simple as the mowing machine and rake could have altered the farmer's life to such an extent that a poet would compose a song about them. But such is the case, and old settlers can supply many other details of the change from their memory of bygone days. They remember, for example, the time when they could not afford to buy carts and would have to load the potatoes, as they dug them up from among the tree stumps and hollows of the burnt land, into home-made wicker baskets. These baskets (*cliabh*) were familiar to them from the days of the primitive agriculture that they had carried on in Scotland. They would hang one on each side of a horse on a straddle (*srathair*), also home-made, and thus carry home their produce pannier-style. The method may not seem unduly arduous, and, unquestionably, it is picturesque, but the construction of each hand-woven basket required several hours of labour now unnecessary.

Fishing methods were equally primitive. All nets were knit by hand. As recently as sixty years ago the Cape Breton fishermen did not even use lobster traps. Instead they lowered a huge metal hoop to the bottom of the sea; to this was attached a net, in the centre of which a codfish head was tied for bait. When several lobsters had gathered around the bait, the hoop was swiftly lifted by the leader attached to it, and the fisherman thus caught any lobsters that were too slow-witted or clumsy to scuttle off the net before it reached the surface. The modern lobster-man with his power boat, carefully constructed traps, and speedy trap-hauler would not relish a return to these good old days.

Farming and fishing became businesses. The only drawback to the change was that the machinery necessary for the business required cash and sometimes took more than it ever seemed to repay. The problem of the countryman was no longer what it had been in Scotland and in the New World during pioneering days—How can we get enough to eat? With the arrival of machinery, the perpetual question became—How can we pay what we owe?

The cash basis affected the life of the housewife as well as her husband's. Her work became simpler. She now could buy the

things she used to make. Labour-saving devices had been accepted by the men for their work as a matter of course, and
eventually they were accepted in the woman's sphere also, although during the period of transition from the old method to
the new, the women-folk suffered considerable criticism. The
simplification of man's work was apparently, in man's judgment,
acceptable as a benefaction of God; the simplification of woman's
work was suspected as the Devil's sinister temptation to sloth.
One of the Gaelic poets in Cape Breton, Kenneth Ferguson,
speaks reproachfully of the change wrought by mail-order
houses:

> Cha b' e Eaton fear ar n-earb-sa
> Chum ar comhdach a bhith dearbhte,
> Ach na mathraichean neo-chearbach
> Le 'n cuid dhealg 's a' gheamhradh.
>
> Ach dh' fhalbh an t-am ud, us cha till e,
> Us dh' fhaodadh nach na's fhearr tha cintinn:
> Saoghal bras air bhoil le riomhadh,
> Us mnathan sgith a' dannsa.[19]

It wasn't Eaton's we depended on to keep us supplied with clothing,
but industrious mothers with their knitting-needles in the winter.

But that time has gone, and it won't return, and probably the world
isn't growing any better—an impetuous world in a frenzy for finery,
and the women tired out with dancing.

Murdoch Morrison is no kinder to the ladies. He was born in
1842, and his songs were written down from his dictation in
1928, so that he had lived through the two periods, the period
of home industry and the period of the mail-order catalogue.
He tells us:

> Tha na boirionnach a th' ann
> Gu math cosgail aig gach am;
> Gu b' e de a thig 'n an ceann,
> Bidh sannt ac' air an comhnuidh.
>
> Ach innsidh mise dhuibhse 'n fhirinn—
> Creidibh i 's na deadaibh 'diteadh—
> Gur e 'n leabhar mor aig Eaton
> 'Dh' fhag na miltean leomach.[20]

The present-day women are certainly extravagant every time; whatever thing comes into their head, they'll always have a lust for it.

But I'll tell you the truth (believe it, and don't contradict it): it's
Eaton's big catalogue that left thousands so conceited.

Apparently there is a certain amount of truth in what old Murdoch said, although he may have exaggerated his point a little. Home-made clothing went so entirely out of fashion that the man who would wear it had to be willing to face the ridicule of his neighbours. An old Cape Breton school-teacher, now in his eighties, remarking on the small salary he used to earn, added, "Of course, I could wear home-spun in those days. Clothing didn't cost me anything then, but after my time if a teacher had appeared in home-spun in the school-house the children would have driven him out." The sturdy home-spun was no longer the respected symbol of virtuous woman's industry; now it was scorned by the rising generation as the symbol of outmoded poverty.

The countryman and his wife were not the only people affected by the changed mode of living on this continent. A third class was affected—the local artisans. Even in the most primitive communities in the Highlands and Islands the people had employed local handy men who specialized each in some craft. As society stabilized itself in the New World, the settlement gathered around itself a clergyman, a doctor, a teacher, a storekeeper, and a group of artisans. Each district was provided with a shoemaker and a tailor, who often travelled from house to house in the traditional Scottish manner. Each district had its own grist-mill and saw-mill. Villages often had both a cabinet-maker and a carriage-maker, sometimes a boat-builder, and always a blacksmith. Most of these specialists are now gone. The blacksmith alone retains his standing in the community, and even he is yielding place to the garage mechanic. An occupational directory of Nova Scotia for the year 1864 presents a very different picture of the Highland communities from that of today. In Whycocomagh, for instance (which at that time had a population of about 1,800),[21] besides the inevitable teacher, innkeepers, and merchants, we find a shipwright, a carriage-maker, a wheelwright, a tanner, two millers, two blacksmiths, and two tailors.[22] A later directory for the year 1868 shows the village still as well provided and enumerates, in addition to the previous list, one dyer.[23] In Whycocomagh today, one would seek in vain for such craftsmen except the blacksmith.

Other districts itemized in the directories show the same decline. All were once well supplied with the service of local craftsmen. Sometimes one craft predominated, sometimes another. In North Gut St. Ann's, for instance, we find no less than five weavers listed for the year 1864.[24] On the mainland of Nova Scotia during the same period we find in the St. Andrew's district seven carpenters, six shoemakers, three ship-carpenters, three tailors, two masons, two millwrights, two carriage-makers, two tanners, and a surveyor.[25]

Now, for various reasons, these local artisans are vanished. There is, for instance, no longer any need for the services of the carriage-maker. And in almost all the rural districts the population has decreased so much that there may often not be sufficient local business for a full-time carpenter. But the main reasons adduced by local residents for the change are the development of mass machine production, the growth of large organized and centralized businesses, and the introduction of the mail-order system. The local industries pined away in the competition against the larger producer, who offered a more showy article to the public than the local artisan could produce, and who by the hypnotism of advertising persuaded an impressionable public to judge what they bought in terms of the latest fashion.

As early as 1809 the Reverend James MacGregor foresaw that in Pictou County the self-reliant character of the pioneer was threatened by "the avarice, the luxury, the show, and the glittering toys" introduced by the inrush of merchants and traders from England and the south of Scotland.[26] His fears were well grounded, and there are Nova Scotians today who ascribe the decline of rural prosperity to the harm wrought by the much more pervasive and seductive high-pressure salesmanship of the big business that grew to power after his time.[27] The benefits afforded to the countryman by the new system have been manifold: he has been released from the unending round of toil necessary to the peasant who feeds, clothes, and houses himself unaided; he may enrol the services of big business to supply him with every imaginable item that he needs. But he must himself become a skilful economist. Many farms today might not be lying idle if the owners had not so readily accepted the many machine-made products offered them and then found that all their land and cattle could not yield returns enough to pay the price.

Those who work the land and fish the seas are, as the rural reformers point out, the sustainers of civilization; without the food which they provide, mankind could not survive. Whatever corrupts and weakens them, corrupts and weakens civilization itself. The peasant immigrants have enjoyed a fairy-tale career from poverty to riches, from need to luxury, but luxury is a greedy and extravagant mistress.

9

The Lure of the City

THE FOLKWAYS of the Highland settlers yielded place to the machine, and the rural settlements lost their population to the modern city which the machine created. The dominant desire of the settlers had been to gain possession of land which they could call their own, to make an independent living on it, and to raise families in the security offered by rural life. Within two or three generations the descendants of such pioneers sought new goals.

The results of this change are strikingly evident within the various Highland settlements of Cape Breton.[1] One may now drive for many miles along country roads and see nothing but abandoned pasture land covered over with spruce trees, with here and there the crumbling remains of a barn or farm-house. Yet fifty years ago every inch of the way led past cultivated land, dotted with comfortable farm-houses. Every farm once supported a large family, and the now neglected property was valued so highly that a boundary dispute might be the cause of a bitter feud between the kindliest of neighbours.

The reasons for this change are numerous. One can easily understand why the children who entered the professions should leave their old homes; they were inevitably tempted to move to the place where they could find the best opportunity for their talents. But why the many men and women without any special training abandoned farming or fishing settlements in favour of the unknown is a phenomenon that demands a fuller explanation.

In a study written in the eighteen-eighties on the Highland settlements in Stormont and Glengarry counties, Ontario, where a process of migration similar to that in Cape Breton was taking place, George Sandfield MacDonald admitted that many of the finest Gaels had left their settled country homes.[2] They were taking up a more stirring life, he explained, as lumbermen in the forests of Michigan, as settlers on the prairies of Minnesota, as construction men on the new railways, and as farmers in North Dakota, because the quietness of their old settlements did not suit their "impetuous and restless dispositions." Their voluntary abandonment of their native home was a healthy symptom of their energy.

Perhaps restlessness also affected the people of Nova Scotia, but another factor contributing to the depopulation was—ironically enough—the healthy and rapid increase in population within the families of settlers. Eventually, we must suppose, the farms became overcrowded and overburdened and could no longer feed so many mouths.

The course of events can be easily visualized. The Highland immigrants arrived on the shores of Cape Breton, shipload upon shipload, summer after summer. The first and most fortunate arrivals seized the most promising farm land, the intervales, as they are called locally, the level and luxuriant slopes bordering on river, lake, or sea. The later settlers climbed out through the forest past the already occupied land and found what sites they could in the rear-lands and on the mountain sides. Once settled, the families multiplied prodigiously.

Local histories supply ample illustration. John MacKenzie and his wife Mary, for instance,[3] came from Barra to Christmas Island in 1821, bringing with them their first child. Most of the best front land had been taken, but they were able to buy a hundred-acre farm for £70. It ran from the shores of the Bras d'Or Lakes back through the forest, contained reasonably level and fertile farm land, and—conveniently enough—even had a log-house already built on it, in which they were able to spend the first winter. John found some hay on the property, which he cut by hand with a sickle. He bought two cows and a few sheep, which he supported through the winter on this feed. Within a few years he was able to buy a horse and plough and thus became securely established as a farmer. In due time his wife bore nine more children. Four of the sons raised families on the original property—not to mention the families raised by the daughters—and the total number of children in these four families was thirty-two. Obviously the hundred-acre lot which had appeared such a godsend to John in the first generation when he had just arrived from Scotland with his wife and young baby, no longer offered the same abundant opportunity to the thirty-two grandchildren. As we might expect, the girls of the third generation married and moved away, and most of the boys also left and found a living elsewhere.

Large families such as these strained the farms beyond what they could stand. The soil, worked and reworked without any scientific system, became impoverished under the constant strain of producing food for so many people. The fertility of the burnt lands became only a wondrous memory cherished by the oldest settlers.

At this stage in the life of the communities, presumably, the wholesale abandonment of the farms began. Once the superfluous portion of the growing farm population began to leave, they were followed by the active and energetic who could have remained but were weary of the soil and the land and were eager to taste the pleasures and comfort of city life. The poorest farm lands were the first to lose their population, and they are entirely desolate today; they were the inaccessible spots where none but the land-hungry immigrants last to arrive deigned to settle. There is no real tragedy in the desertion of these impossible situations, but many a beautiful and once productive farm has also been abandoned in the stampede away from the country.

No individual person can be singled out for blame for deserting the countryside, yet those who have remained complain that society as a whole has been seriously unbalanced through depopulation of the rural areas. Unemployment to them seems madness while land lies untended in the country; starvation seems criminal while fertile soil, unsown and unreaped in deserted farming areas, wastes its potential exuberance on weeds.

The extent of migration from the country must have been tremendous, although there is no way to measure it precisely. The ruins of deserted farms do not reveal the total picture, and the only statistics available are difficult to interpret. Without entangling ourselves too deeply in the subtleties of the statistician's art we may, however, sample the population changes in a few of the predominantly Gaelic areas of Cape Breton. The official census of Canada was first taken in 1871, and has been retaken every ten years since that time. Below are the enumerations of the areas selected for the years 1881 and 1941.[4] In 1881 the majority of the settlements reached their maximum and began to decline steadily thereafter; two of the settlements had acquired their maximum population even before that date, while one of them did not reach its maximum until the following census,[5] but 1881 seems to have been the general turning point and has therefore been adopted for the purpose of illustration.

Census district	1881	1941
Judique	2,027	904
Whycocomagh North	1,787	696
Grand Narrows	1,464	852
South-West Margaree	1,246	731
Little Narrows North and South	817	455
South Gut St. Ann's	788	315
North River	768	434
North Shore	697	327
Framboise	680	397
Loch Lomond	437	170

With this shrinkage we may compare the lusty and unfaltering growth of Sydney, the principal industrial town in Cape Breton:

1871	1881	1891	1901	1911	1921	1931	1941
1,700	2,180	2,427	9,909	17,723	22,545	23,089	28,305

Not all, of course, of the Highland descendants who left rural Cape Breton went to the cities. Some enterprising young men travelled west and settled on the new wheat fields; others went as far as the West Coast to engage in the lumbering business. But the city was the goal for the majority, men and women alike.

Those from Nova Scotia and Prince Edward Island were drawn as by a magnet to Boston. Montreal, although on Canadian soil, seemed foreign and uninviting to them because of its French-speaking population; but, during the latter years of the previous century, prosperous Boston with its ready opportunities for employment had all the lure of the fabled El Dorado. There they could escape from the long daily hours of labour on the farm, and find easy work, ready cash, the latest conveniences, and the latest fashions.

Boston became for the Maritimer a symbol of culture and wealth, and the people back home heard its glories sung so often that, overawed, they came to refer to the forty-eight states of the Union as "the Boston States." And even though Boston has enjoyed less prosperous days through the present century, it has continued, because of its geographical accessibility, to serve as a refuge to those who wish to find city employment. One would search in vain today among the Highland settlements in the Maritimes for a native who could not say, "Some of my people are living in Boston."

Many anecdotes are told of the dispersal of the New World Gaels. One of the wandering Gaels from Cape Breton found a position as orderly in a hospital for the insane in Pennsylvania. One day a patient was brought in to this hospital by the police in order that the psychiatrists might find out the cause of his trouble. The man in question was extremely depressed, refused to eat, and would not speak to anyone. The psychiatrists were baffled and locked him up, hoping that time might cure him of his extreme melancholy. The orderly brought in a meal to the patient and spoke cheerfully to him, but the patient showed no signs that he heard a word, and paid no attention to his food. The orderly was about to leave the room when some strange feeling impelled him to turn back again and say in Gaelic, in a cheerful and casual way, "You're not hungry today." The silent patient lifted his head; a smile spread over his wan face; and he burst into a stream of Gaelic in reply to the astonished orderly. He told his story. He had left Cape Breton as a young man; he had worked hard to support an invalid mother; he had run short of money and had suffered a nervous breakdown. He came to feel that everyone was against him. Only when he heard the warming sound of his mother tongue, which he had not heard since he left his home, did his attitude change, and the spell was broken.

It was not without regret that the Gaels left their homes. They would not have been truly Gaels if they had not felt pangs of separation when they parted from the scenes of their childhood.

Something of this feeling is reflected in a song which John V. MacNeil composed when he left his home in Christmas Island and set out for the United States:

Nuair dh' fhag mi taigh mo mhathar
'S a' ghleann 's an deachaidh m' arach,
Bha sneachda geal fo m' shailtean—
Gur anns a' Mhart a dh' fhalbh mi.

Ged bha mo choltas sunndach
Nuair thionndaidh mi mo chul ribh,
Gu'n robh mo chridhe bruite
Ged bha mo shuil gun deargan.[6]

When I left my mother's house and the glen where I was reared, the snow was white under my heels—it was in March I went away.

My looks were cheery when I turned my back on you, yet my heart was breaking, even though my eyes were without redness.

After he reached Boston he used to think with longing of his old home in Marsh Glen:

Gur e mise tha gun phris
'S mi seo am "Baile nam Beans"
'S gun de dhachaidh agam fhin
Ach rum bideach ann an "garret."

Nuair a's motha bhios mo ghruaim
'S mo thoil-intinn fada bhuam,
Thig mi steach a shuidhe suas
'Ghabhail duanag air mo ghalair.

'S ged a bhiodh mo chridhe trom,
'S mi gun sunnd, gu bruite, fann,
Gu'm bu lighich' dhomh 's an am
A bhith thall an Gleann na Maise.[7]

Here I am, an insignificant creature, in Bean Town with no home of my own except a tiny room in the garret.

When my gloom is at its greatest and my pleasure far away, I come in and sit down to sing a song about my affliction.

And should my heart be heavy and I be joyless, wilted, spiritless, to be back in Marsh Glen at such a time would be the physician I need.

Homesick or not, however, John V., like many of his compatriots, did not return to his native glen but tried to make a success of the new life he had adopted. His subsequent career[8] typifies the ideals of the young adventurer of his day. In Boston he became a capable builder. Later he moved to Los Angeles, California, and there through building and investing acquired a fortune which he certainly never could have amassed if he had stayed on his farm. In view of such an example it is not surprising that thousands of other young lads left their homes and were willing to endure life in a garret room.

Most local bards, however, ignored the possibility that the great migration might profit the individual; instead, they lamented the sight of deserted farm-house and neglected fields. Duncan MacDonald composed a song[9] after returning in 1918 to his old homestead at French Road, Cape Breton, and finding the building in ruins. He pictures the scene only briefly, but his emotions are vividly presented:

> Gur mis' tha bronach an seo am onar,
> 'S mi cur gu meorachadh air gach cas;
> 'S e 'n cnocan boidheach, far an robh mi solasach
> An toiseach m' oige, tha 'n diugh 'gam chnamh.
>
> 'S bochd an sgath leam tighinn thun na laraich
> Far an deachaidh m' arach nuair bha mi og;
> Tha cliadain chrasgach an diugh a' fas oirre
> 'S feanntag ard, 's chan fhaigh mi 'n a coir.
>
> Chan eil fardach no maide-laraich
> Far am biodh manran us gaire 's ceol. . . .
>
> An comunn gaolach, a bha mi daonnan
> 'N am measg 's an taobh seo nuair bha mi og,
> Gur e aon duine diubh 's an naoidhnear
> Tha 'n diugh ri fhaotainn, 's chan fhaic mi 'n corr.
>
> 'S e fath mo smaointinn an seo 'n am aonaran
> Mu gach aon a bh' ann sean us og,
> An diugh air sgaoileadh 's gach cearn de'n t-saoghal,
> 'S an roinn a's mo dhiubh a' cnamh fo'n fhod.

Mournful am I here alone, set to thinking about each misfortune; the lovely hill-side, where in the spring-tide of my youth I once was happy, today torments my mind.

It's a sad trial for me to come back to the ruins of the place where I was reared as a boy; tangled burdock is growing over it and tall nettles, and I can't get near the place.

There is now neither shelter nor flooring where once there was gaiety and laughter and music. . . .

Today I can find only one out of nine of the dear comrades whose company I was always in, in the days of my youth here; the others I cannot see.

This is why here in solitude I am brooding about all those, young and old, who used to be here, and who today are scattered to every quarter of the world, and the most of them wasting under the sod.

Sadder than the nostalgia of the returning native is the plight of those who were bereft of neighbours and left almost alone in the country. The bards have spoken also on their behalf. Angus Ban MacFarlane of Margaree, who was a successful farmer and lived in the country to the end of his ninety years of life,[10] speaks regretfully of the depopulation of the nearby settlement of Egypt at the head of Piper's Glen:

> 'S mor am milleadh air an Eipheit
> Na fir ghleusda 'bhith 'g a fagail:
> MacGill-Eathain, MacGill-Fhaolain,
> Us MacEadhmuinn 'threig an t-aite.[11]

Great is the loss to Egypt, the fine men that are leaving it: MacLean, MacLellan, and MacAdam who have deserted the place.

But more than any he misses his friend Neil when he visits Piper's Glen and views the deserted house where once he had been so well entertained:

> Nuair a rainig mi an clireadh
> Anns an robh thu, Neill, a' tamhachd,
> Fhuair mi 'n fhardach air a dunadh;
> Shil mo shuilean, 's cha bu nar dhomh.
>
> Nuair a chruinnicheadh na h-eolaich
> Staigh 'nad sheomar, mar bu ghnath leo,
> Gu'm biodh cridhealas gu leor ann,
> 'S gheibhte ceol us orain Ghaidhlig.
>
> Dh' fhalbh thu bhuainn a Gleann a' Phiobair';
> Chuir sin mighean air mo nadur.
> 'S ann ort fhein 's air do chuid cloinne
> 'Chaidh a shloinneadh, tha iad ag raitinn.
>
> Seinnidh Iain grinn a' phiob dhuit;
> Seinnidh Sin' i agus Tearlach,
> Eachann, Floiri, agus Seumas,
> Mary Jane, us May, us Searlot.

When I reached the clearing where you were living, Neil, I found the house locked up; the tears came to my eyes, as well they might.

When friends would gather in your room as they used to like to, there would be merriment a-plenty and music and Gaelic songs.

You have gone away from us from Piper's Glen, and that sheds gloom on my spirits; it was after you and your children that the glen was named, they say.

Handsome John can play the pipes for you; Jean can play them and Charlie; Hector, Flora, and James, Mary Jane, and May, and Charlotte.

In the chorus of the song he sums up his melancholy at the loss of such a neighbour:

> Ho gur misde, he gur misde,
> Ho gur misde leam mar tha 'chuis;
> 'S misde leam gu'n d' rinn thu gluasad
> Null gu tir a' ghuail a thamhachd.

Oh, I'm the worse; Oh, I'm the worse; Oh, I'm the worse as things have turned; I'm the worse since you have moved away to stay in the country of coal.

Occasionally a country-loving bard poses the sage question to those who have exchanged the farm for the city life, "Are you any the better of the change?" But very few undertake to supply an answer. One of the rare treatments of the problem[12] comes from a highly educated Gael, Joseph D. MacKinnon, who was at one time principal of the Glace Bay High School in Cape Breton. Living as he did in the midst of a network of coal-mining towns, he knew intimately the conditions to which his fellow Gaels were condemned when they hopefully took up mining as a career. His cry to them is, "Return to the farm":

> O! nach bochd do Ghaidheal fhallain
> Fuireach anns an aite seo
>
> 'Bhith 'n a thraill bho Luan gu Sathurn
> Aig aintighearnan fo sailtean,
>
> Nuair a dh' fhaodadh e bhi sona
> Air baile farsuing aluinn
>
> Le crodh laoidh, caoirich gheala,
> Cearcan, eich, 's car dh' fhaoit',
>
> Obair ghlan air uachdar talamh,
> Seach toll dubh an amhraidh.

Oh, isn't it a shame for a healthy Gael living in this place to be a
slave from Monday to Saturday under the heels of tyrants, when
he could be happy on a handsome spreading farm with milk-cows,
white sheep, hens, horses, and perhaps a car, and clean work on the
surface of the earth, rather than in the black pit of misery.

But the lamentations of poets seldom change the course of
history. Heedless of songs, the Gaels submerged themselves in
distant industrial and business centres of the machine-age world.
They were apparently satisfied with their new setting and did
not seem to miss the independence and self-sufficiency of the
farmer's life, which they had to surrender when they engaged
themselves in the service of an employer. Ironically, however,
some of those remaining in the country began to feel inferior and
act deferentially or even apologetically when their prosperous
city cousins came back to visit them.

In the judgment of the rural folk tradition, the men who mi-
grated to the city became pompous, the women snobbish, and
girls excessively stylish. Not merely did the expatriates disown
the Gaelic language, learned from the lips of their mothers; those
who went to Boston even turned against their own melodious
dialect of English, which still characterizes the Gaels of Cape
Breton, affecting in its place an exaggerated elegance of speech
and a nasal, drawling accent which they considered to be a model
of correct Bostonian speech. Although such behaviour was
adopted probably only by an offensive minority, the local bards
of course censured it indignantly. D. D. MacFarlane, in a song
first published in 1897,[13] says in praise of one of the local girls
of Margaree:

> Ged bha thu cuairt feadh nan Staidean Aonaicht',
> Cha d' thug sin smaointean bha faoin 'nad cheann,
> Thu soitheamh, ciallach, ro-chiuin am briathran,
> Mar chleachd thu riamh mu'n do thriall thu ann.

> Although you went for a trip to the United States, that didn't put
> foolish ideas in your head; you are as mannerly and sensible and as
> quiet in your speech as ever you were before you went there.

The implication of the praise is clearly that the girl was exceptional, and that the many others who went on the same trip
were not so unspoiled when they returned. In a sprightly letter

to *Mac-Talla*, written in August, 1894,[14] when numbers of Cape Breton expatriates were returning home for the summer months to their native community, Framboise, a local observer remarked:

> Tha sinn fìor thoilichte ann a bhith 'g innse gu bheil moran de'n oigridh againn 'n ar measg dhachaidh as na Staidean. Chan urrainn duinn a radh gu bheil iad uile cho dreachmhor 's a bha iad mu'n d' fhalbh iad, ach neo-air-thaing deagh chomhdach, agus, tha sinn an dochas, gliog math 'n an sporain.

> Tha siud gle mhath 'n a aite fhein, gidheadh, tha beagan agam 'n an aghaidh, agus 's e seo e: an dimeas a tha cuid dhiubh a' deanamh air a' Ghailig. Iad sin a labhradh a' Ghaidhlig gu math mu'n d' fhalbh iad, 's ann tha iad a nise, an deigh dhaibh a bhith beagan bhliadhnaichean air falbh, ma's fior, air a diochuimhneachadh. Nuair a chomhlaicheas mi iad le cainnt bhinn bhlasda mo mhathar, nach ann a their iad rium, "No Gaelic!" Ach cumaidh mise 'Ghailig riutha, 's ma thuigeas iad mi, 's math, 's mur tuig, chan eil comas air.

> We're very glad to say that many of our young people are home from the States among us. We can't say that they're all as presentable as they were before they left, but at least they are well dressed and, we hope, have a good clink in their purses.

> That is very good in its proper place, but I have something against them, and it is this: the contempt with which some of them are treating Gaelic. Those who used to speak Gaelic well before they left have now, after being away for a few years, ostensibly forgotten it. When I greet them with the rich, sweet language of my mother, what do they say to me but "No Gaelic!" But I keep the Gaelic at them, and if they understand, all's well, and if they don't, it can't be helped.

This antipathy to the mother tongue, introduced by the city-bred Gaels, affected the country people also and struck deep at the roots of the language. Garret MacDonald of North River Meadow, Cape Breton, sums up quaintly[15] the degraded position that Gaelic came to occupy even in the country:

> Saoilidh mi gur amadanachd
> Do neach a bhith cho starnail
> Ged bhiodh e 's na Staidean bliadhna
> Gu'n diochuimhnich e a' Ghaidhlig.

> Tha moran an ar duthaich—
> Tha mi 'n duil gu bheil e nair' dhaibh—
> Gun Bheurla aca chuireadh a mach an cu,
> 'S cha chan iad aon ghuth Ghaidhlig.

I consider it foolishness for anyone to be so stuck-up, because he'd been in the States for a year, that he should forget his Gaelic.

There are many in our land (I think it's a disgrace for them) without English enough to put the dog out who won't speak one word of Gaelic.

To explain the growth of this fierce contempt for the mother tongue, amateur sociologists among the Gaels point out that the young people who grew up in the pioneering communities unwittingly tended to associate the Gaelic language which they heard at that time with the incessant toil, hardship, and scarcity peculiar to primitive conditions. When they went to the city, the universal language was English, while Gaelic was unknown; and the standard of living there was inconceivably superior to what they had known. Hence Gaelic came to be considered the language of poverty and ignorance and was therefore despised, while English was regarded as the language of refinement and culture and therefore cherished.

Not everyone, however, adopted this unreflective attitude towards Gaelic. As the people travelled more extensively, they began to appraise the apparent glitter of the city more shrewdly and came to realize there was nothing contemptible in the old and honest way of life on the farm and nothing shameful about their ancient language. Gaels in distant cities began to take pride in their language, so that now they flock to listen to a Gaelic play or concert or to attend a Gaelic church service. In Boston there are two Protestant churches—the United Presbyterian Church and the Scotch Presbyterian Church—which have gathered congregations of four hundred or more for services in Gaelic. Many members of both are Gaelic-speaking people who have come, not from Scotland, but from the Gaelic settlements of Canada—especially from Prince Edward Island and from Nova Scotia. A street intersection between the two churches became so popular as a meeting place for the members of both congregations that they named the place "Scotch corner." There (until quite recently) the people would gather after service, and the subject of their conversation was usually news from the old home, and the language they spoke, as often as not, was Gaelic. The Gaels have merged into the stream of North American city life, but they still retain a feeling of individuality, a love for their own traditions, and a memory of their own unique origin.

They retain also an instinctive feeling of attachment to the countryside. The bards do not respond to city life, not because in that new environment they have forgotten their mother tongue or lost their command of poetry but because they lack the stimulus provided to their forefathers for so many generations by the simple joys and sorrows of country life.

10

Gaelic in Cape Breton

THE GREAT MIGRATION from Nova Scotia, though extensive, has not stripped the Highland settlements entirely of their original stock. In Cape Breton especially there are still many districts where the people are descended from the first Highland settlers without any new racial mixture acquired on this side of the Atlantic. These descendants are, indeed, of as pure stock as any in the remotest islands of the Hebrides or loneliest glens in the Highlands. In Cape Breton, as nowhere else, one can study the fusion of the Old World and the New World among these people. Their traditions and their attitudes are still Highland; their way of life has been adapted through necessity to conditions in Canada.

To the casual tourist the first sign of the Highland nature of the communities in Cape Breton is the preponderance of the old Scottish clan names. One clan predominates in one community; another in the next. In 1942 at the Baddeck Bay school eleven of the fourteen pupils, the teacher, two of the retiring trustees and all three of the incoming trustees were MacLeods.[1] The island of Barra in Scotland is traditionally the rallying ground of the MacNeil clan, yet there are more MacNeils in one of the polling sections in Victoria County, Cape Breton, than may be found in all Barra.[2]

The high frequency of certain clan names in a district has resulted in the preservation of the old Highland system of naming people. Obviously in a community such as Baddeck Bay the expression "Mr. MacLeod" is meaningless, and as ambiguous as the term "Mr. MacNeil" would be in Iona. Even the terms "John MacLeod" and "James MacNeil" would not help very considerably to clear away confusion in a place where there might be fifteen "John MacLeods" or twenty "James MacNeils."

The accepted method of designating people under these circumstances is a traditional Highland device. The head of the house is called by his first name followed by an identifying name, usually either the first name of his father or a nickname. If, for instance, the first name of the head of the house is Neil and his father's name was James, then, regardless of what his last name may be, he is universally known in the neighbourhood as Neil Jim. With his name thus established without any ambiguity, the naming of the other members of his household becomes very simple. His wife is spoken of as Mrs. Neil Jim; his children, Malcolm and Mary, let us say, are identified, in a euphonious combination of names, as Malcolm Neil Jim and Mary Neil Jim.

Understanding this system, a stranger may still be mystified as to the identity of people mentioned in conversation unless he understands Gaelic, for even in an English conversation the names of people are often rendered in Gaelic. The title Neil Jim when expressed in Gaelic becomes something which to the ear of an English-speaking person seems both strange and unexpected. As may be seen from the following chart, the Gaelic form of the name Neil, spelled *Niall*, approximates in pronunciation the English form. James is Seumas, approximately like the two English words "shame us." But when the two names are put together, expressing the idea, "Neil son of James," the second name is put into the genitive case, meaning "of James," and is pronounced in another manner. The first syllable might be represented as "hame" to rime with "fame"; the second syllable, as "ish" to rime with "dish."

Language	*Son*	*Father*	*Identifying name*
English	Neil	James	Neil Jim
Gaelic (written)	Niall	Seumas	Niall Sheumais
(pronounced)	"Neil"	"shame us"	"Neil hame-ish"

Families sometimes become identified with a nickname instead of the traditional father-and-son title. One of the MacNeils of Iona came to be known as "John Banker," not because of any connection with the banking business but because for many years he had engaged in fishing off the Grand Banks. Such names often cling to families long after the original reason for them has disappeared. One of the many MacNeil families settled around the Bras d'Or Lakes is descended from Rory MacNeil, who was a piper to the laird of Barra in Scotland;[3] these MacNeils in the fifth, sixth, and seventh generations are still spoken of as the Pipers, although the musical art has not survived among them. Even more perverse is the case of the Ridge MacDonalds. Allan MacDonald emigrated from Lochaber in 1816 and settled in Cape Breton on the ridge of the Mabou Mountain; because of the place where he lived he was dubbed locally "Allan the Ridge."[4] Later he moved to South River in Antigonish County, but the name clung to him and descended to his son, "Alec the Ridge," and even to his grandson, who is known today as "Angus the Ridge."

The degree to which the people have remained truly Highland may be measured by their retention of the Gaelic language. Only by retaining their language can the people preserve their oral traditions and their music; when they lose the language they lose with it much that marks them off from the other people settled in the New World. For this reason Cape Breton may be considered the last strong-hold of the old Gaels.

Gaelic was once very strong in all the larger Highland settlements in North America. In North Carolina even the Negro servants learned the language from their masters—a circumstance that greatly confused an old Highland lady when she landed on the shores of America. As she disembarked at the wharf, she was delighted to hear two men conversing in Gaelic. Assuming by their speech that they must inevitably be fellow Highlanders, she came nearer, only to discover that their skin was black. Then she knew that her worst forebodings about the climate of the South were not unfounded and cried out in horror, "A Dhia nan gras, am fas sinn uile mar sin?" (O God of mercy, are we all going to turn black like that?)[5]

Gaelic gradually died out among the descendants of these people, both black and white. The last Gaelic sermon preached in North Carolina was delivered in Galatin, Cumberland County, in 1860. By that time only the old people in the community understood the language.[6]

Gaelic has lasted more successfully in Ontario and in Prince Edward Island and on the mainland of Nova Scotia. In all the Canadian Gaelic settlements there are usually some old people who can recall their Gaelic and some younger who understand the language without being able to speak it, but in none of these places will one easily find families where both young and old habitually converse together in the ancient tongue. It is in the island of Cape Breton that the language is best preserved.

A hundred years and more have gone by since the Highland settlers came out from Scotland to Cape Breton, and those who could speak only Gaelic and knew no English have now almost all passed away, even in the most remote country settlements. This fact has weakened Gaelic wherever non-Gaelic-speaking people have settled among the Gaels. At one time while Gaels who knew no English still survived, any new-comer to a Highland community who could not speak Gaelic must of necessity learn the language in order to converse with the people; now the entire community can adapt itself to such an intruder and will speak English for his benefit. In the eighteen-hundreds Thomas Bryden came out from England; he married a girl of Barra stock and settled with her in Piper's Cove, Cape Breton.[7] He could speak no Gaelic, and she could speak no English. Their descendants, however, living in a Gaelic community spoke little else but Gaelic, and those of the third generation today who live in Cape Breton are still fluent in their grandmother's language. A few Strachans from Aberdeenshire (where Gaelic is not spoken) settled in the neighbourhood of Framboise, Cape Breton; one of them was a music teacher by profession. All their descendants became fluent Gaelic speakers; and several of them inherited their forefather's gift for music and developed a real talent for singing the Gaelic songs which they learned from their neighbours.

The most celebrated case in Cape Breton of non-Gaelic-speaking persons adopting the language is that of John and George Maxwell, Negro twins.[8] The father of these twins was adopted when a child by a Gaelic-speaking sea-captain whose home was in Cape Breton. Here the boy quickly and inevitably learned Gaelic—the language of the household and of the neighbourhood. When he married he continued to use Gaelic in his own home, and thus his twin sons learned the language. John settled in Malagawatch and died some twenty years ago. His twin brother, George, settled in Whycocomagh and died in 1936 when in his seventies. According to report he always enjoyed speaking Gaelic and sang the Gaelic songs enthusiastically. Since Negroes are much more rare in Cape Breton than in North Carolina, the Maxwell twins are remembered as a sort of monument to the language.

Gaelic today can be said to flourish only in country districts where there has been no intrusion of non-Gaelic-speaking people. Communities which have become mixed with those whose only language is English are now no longer able to assimilate Brydens, and Strachans, and Maxwells as they did fifty years ago. There are, however, many thriving Gaelic communities remaining. There is Egypt at the head of Piper's Glen, where the business of the annual school meeting is still conducted in Gaelic. There is North River, where many families still conduct their daily worship in Gaelic and where at least one family retains the custom of precenting and singing the Gaelic psalms each morning and evening at family worship. There is Wreck Cove; a minister wrote concerning the people there that "they live, move, and have their being in the language; indeed, they think in it and dream in it, and, if they swear, they do that also in Gaelic."[9]

In Cape Breton, Gaelic is, generally speaking, preserved in the country and forgotten in the town. Perhaps the innate politeness of the Gael makes him reticent to use his native tongue in the city amid those who do not understand the language. Ardent lovers of Gaelic find fault with themselves and their fellow Gaels for the exercise of such undue modesty on behalf of people who are, after all, only passing strangers. They point out that on the side-walk or in the street-cars in a large town such as Sydney you may hear Chinamen conversing together unabashed in Chinese; Italians, Frenchmen, Hungarians, and Syrians, each talking his own language; yet you will rarely if ever hear a Gael speaking Gaelic with a friend. The old sense of shame for the language also inhibits its use. A young man at a dance in one of the Cape Breton towns might very easily be insulted if anyone addressed him in Gaelic, no matter how frequently he might speak it at home. Since their language is the speech of a minority, the members of that minority have come to feel (as so often happens in North America) that it is inferior to the language used by the majority around them.

Will Gaelic die in Cape Breton? This question is often asked, both by those who themselves speak the language, and by those who do not but are attracted to it by the curiosity of its history. The answer seems to be largely dependent on the future of the rural Gaelic communities. The language is not likely to survive in the cities. Large and appreciative audiences will gather in Sydney or Glace Bay to listen to a Gaelic concert or watch a Gaelic play; but the children in these towns are not learning the language from their parents. It is in places such as Egypt and North River and Wreck Cove that the young learn the language from the lips of the old and continue to use it. So long as such communities preserve a high birth rate, a supply of Gaelic-speakers is ensured.

There are hidden forces at work corrupting and weakening the old language of the Gael. The language has been much abused, and even those who love it have been affected by these attacks. A young Sydney man recollects that when he first went to school, not many years ago, the teacher angrily told the children who spoke Gaelic among themselves that what they were speaking was not a language but only a "lingo." His slander, meaningless though it was, must have certainly shaken the faith of his scholars in their mother tongue, for a child, no matter how independent, inevitably tends to give some heed to the utterances of his teacher.

The Highland emigrants from each particular district of Scotland settled in groups together when they came to Cape Breton. Thus Barra men settled around Iona; Lewis men settled around St. Ann's Bay; North Uist people, around Mira Ferry; South Uist people, around Grand Mira; and so on. The people of these clannish settlements naturally preserved the particular dialect of Gaelic that the first settlers brought with them from their own individual region of the Highlands and Islands. Accordingly, today, more than a hundred years later, the offspring of these settlers still speak Gaelic with a Lewis or a Barra or a North Uist or a South Uist accent, depending on the locality in which they were reared. In a place so small as Cape Breton whenever they move away from their own locality they hear a different dialect of Gaelic, and in some cases the dialect is so different from their own that they have difficulty in understanding it correctly. This circumstance tends to discourage the enthusiasm of some Gaelic speakers, who, not appreciating the universality of dialect cleavage, complain that the tongue they speak is not a respectable language but a mere "lingo."

Present-day Gaelic speakers also complain that their vocabulary is becoming impoverished and that the rich language of the first settlers is a thing of the past. Once the old folk-tales and folk-songs and classical poems brought from Scotland formed a sort of treasury of expressive diction, but since these have lost currency few people now possess the key to this word-hoard, and so the picturesque language is forgotten, and only the more common-place vocabulary of conversation remains. The elevated language of the Gaelic sermon also is now seldom heard. Few Gaels read enough of their mother tongue to introduce new expressions into the daily speech of their community or to restore forgotten words. Words depend for their survival only on the everyday conversation between one Gael and another.

The factor which most distresses the Gaels, however, is the way in which English words and expressions have crept into their mother tongue. They ruefully confess that their Gaelic has become "half English and half Gaelic." One hears this apology time and time again in Cape Breton. There are two legitimate reasons for this degeneration of the language and a third reason, not legitimate. In the first place, there are many terms in English for which there never was any Gaelic equivalent. Some things known to the civilization of England never penetrated to the less sophisticated Highlands and Islands of Scotland. In England the prune, to choose a humble illustration, has been recognized as an item of diet for the last 600 years; and the banana and tomato, for the last 350 years;[10] but these domestic luxuries were so little known among the Highlanders, even as late as the period of emigration from Scotland to the New World, that they knew no word in their mother tongue by which to describe them. Household equipment now so familiar as baking powder and the kitchen stove were then known neither in their houses nor in their language. The children knew nothing about candy. The men never troubled themselves about unobtainable building material such as brick or labour-saving devices such as derricks. Naturally enough the Gaels had no word in their language for all these random articles—tomatoes, prunes, bananas, baking powder, stoves, candy, bricks, and derricks—and when these nameless innovations came into the ken and daily use of the settlers, they adopted the convenient English word for each of them and used that even in Gaelic conversation.

In the second place, after the settlers had lived for some time in the New World, they began to meet all the new inventions of our machine age: first trains, then automobiles, and electrical devices, and finally aeroplanes. New inventions require new words; the English language rapidly coined the necessary additions to its stock of words, and this new vocabulary was incorporated wholesale from English by the Gaelic speakers into their mother tongue. Some Gaels, particularly in Scotland, tried to combat this inrush of foreign words into their language and contrived native terms to correspond to the English,[11] such as *carbad-iaruinn* (iron chariot) for "train," or *cagar-cein* (distant whisperer) for "telephone." But these terms have never gained popularity with the ordinary Gaelic speaker in the New World. A few of the well educated, particularly the clergy, may adopt them, but the "train" and the "phone" are just that to the majority of people when they speak Gaelic.

The third reason for the introduction of English words is simply negligence. The Gaelic speakers read English in the newspapers and hear English on the radio to such an extent that, even if they hear Gaelic around them every day and speak the language habitually, English words often come to their tongue more readily than the corresponding native word. You may hear a dignified old Highland lady tell her friend, "Bha upset stomach aice" (She had an upset stomach), when she could name the distress quite as poignantly in Gaelic. On a stormy day, a man will say of the weather, "Tha i tough" (It's tough), when there are any number of satisfying Gaelic adjectives with which he could vilify the elements. There is no consistency about the use of these English substitutes. One day a man will ask, "Am bheil thu busy?" (Are you busy?), using the English adjective; the next day he may say, "Am bheil thu trang?" using the correct Gaelic adjecti/e.

Occasionally the English words borrowed add a certain quaintness to the Gaelic. A story is told of a conversation between two Gaelic-speaking Cape Bretoners. One of them, a Catholic, was on his death bed. His friend, who was a Protestant, wished to console the dying man, so he asked him in Gaelic whether he might offer up a prayer for him. "Certainly," answered the Catholic. "Well," asked the Protestant, "shall I compose a prayer of my own for you or recite the Lord's Prayer?" "Oh, the Lord's Prayer, the Lord's Prayer," answered the invalid, and then he added with a happy smile, "Tha e cho snog." (It is so snug.) Presumably, he felt instinctively that no purely Gaelic term could characterize the comforting words of the Lord's Prayer so well as the expressive adjective which he borrowed from the English.

There is a certain quaintness also about the manner in which English words are made to conform to the patterns of Gaelic grammar. One who knew nothing of Gaelic might not readily recognize that he was listening to a familiar English word when he distinguished in the midst of a Gaelic conversation something that sounded like "smoke-ug." "Smoke-ug" (spelt in Gaelic *smokeadh*) simply means "smoking." The Gael forms a participle out of the English word "smoke" by adding the usual Gaelic suffix *-adh*. Even more puzzling is to hear about a "hection-man." "Hection" is a permutation of the familiar English word "section." The Gael has been speaking about some friend, perhaps, who was working on the railroad and has said of him, "Bha e 'n a (s)hection-man an uraidh." (He was a sectionman last year.) Even though the word has been borrowed from English, the initial "s" sound in this grammatical context has been changed to an "h" sound in conformity to an inexorable law of the language.

With the exception of the negligent use of English words in cases where a perfectly good Gaelic word could be used, the Gaels have no real cause for shame that they have borrowed necessary words now and then from English. After all, no language ever plundered vocabulary so recklessly as the English, and it is only fair that the old pirate should disgorge some of its booty to a needy cousin. But the conscientious lovers of the Gaelic language will not be consoled by this reflection; they are convinced that their language has lost something of its ancient grandeur when it stoops to borrowing.

The obvious solution to the decline of Gaelic in an alien land is to teach the language in schools to the children of Gaelic-speaking parents. This plan has never lacked advocates. As long ago as 1879 John A. Morrison, the Member of Parliament for Victoria County, Cape Breton, addressed an appeal to the Nova Scotia House of Assembly on behalf of the teaching of Gaelic.[12] His fellow members must have been somewhat startled when he began the address, for he delivered it entirely in the language whose cause he was supporting—Gaelic. And those who understood what he was saying must have been impressed by the fervour of his plea. During their annual session the House had debated the question of raising funds for the teaching of French in the provincial schools—always a touchy subject in Canada. Alluding to this debate in the course of his speech, the Honourable John A. said:

> 'S i 'Ghaidhlig a' chainnt a bha aig Adhamh 's a' Gharadh. 'S i a' chainnt a bha aig na baird 's na seanachaidh 's na linntean cian a chaidh seachad, agus feumar a cumail suas anns na sgoiltean; agus ma bhios tasdan air 'fhaotainn air-son cainnt nam Frangach a chumail suas, biodh deich tasdain air-son na Gaidhlig urramaich.

> It is Gaelic that was the language of Adam in the Garden. It is the language that the bards and story-tellers used in the generations that have passed long since, and it must be kept up in the schools; and if a shilling is to be found for keeping up French, let there be ten shillings for the venerable Gaelic.

If other Gaels in the New World had shared this enthusiasm for the language, it would surely have been adopted in the school curriculum that very day. But there were many difficulties in the way. Education is often obliged to concern itself more with the things of this world than with abstract ideals. At that time many Gaels did not wish their children to waste time on the language. They wished them to learn English well so that they could succeed in the world, and to study all the "practical" subjects available. Stern realism was more important to them than sentiment and intangible cultural motives. Even the various colleges where Gaelic has been taught from time to time, such as St. Francis Xavier and Dalhousie in Nova Scotia, and Knox and Queen's in Ontario, have found that Gaelic-speaking students would like to study their mother tongue but have not felt that they could sacrifice any of the routine courses of study in order to do so.

The time came when the Gaels of Nova Scotia won recognition for their language by the school authorities. In 1921 the provincial department of education admitted the language as an optional subject on the curriculum.[13] Since that time any school may teach Gaelic, providing that students elect to study the language and the trustees can find a qualified teacher. The immediate results from this apparent triumph were negligible, not so much because of the lack of willing students but because of the difficulty of finding competent teachers. Any enthusiastic teacher could stir up the interest of students to devote some of their time to the language, but who will be the teacher? In the rural communities of Cape Breton, where the most apt students would be found, the teacher is probably an eighteen-year-old girl who has twenty students to look after in a one-room schoolhouse, students whose ages vary from perhaps seven to fifteen, and whose grades number from one to ten. She can hardly be expected to be able to devote much time or energy to teaching a language which she has never studied, even supposing that she speaks Gaelic fluently.

Gaelic grammar and spelling cannot, of course, be mastered over night. English-speaking people have inherited a long tradition of studying their own mother tongue; yet even the university graduate who has devoted his attention to its intricacies during twelve years of school and four years of college furtively consults a dictionary to verify the spelling of quite simple English words and hesitates about grammatical usage. How much harder must this process of learning be then for people

who have always been discouraged from studying their own
language! Gaelic, however, is not, at least in orthography, quite
so capricious as English. It would be by no means impossible for
an active training programme to raise teachers to a fair compe-
tence, and it may be that the recent appointment (1950) of
Major C. I. N. MacLeod as Gaelic Adviser in the Division of
Adult Education[14] will give the language the educational status
in Nova Scotian schools which it deserves.

The study of the language has, moreover, received encouragement in Cape Breton through the founding of a Gaelic College.
A Presbyterian minister, the Reverend A. W. R. MacKenzie,
persuaded a considerable number of people of Scottish descent,
both Highland and Lowland, to raise a fund for the purpose of
fostering Highland traditions in Cape Breton. He bought a
picturesque point of land in St. Ann's Bay and erected a large
log cabin to serve both as a museum of settlers' relics and as a
class-room for the study of Gaelic. This college was opened in
the summer of 1939, and in subsequent summers since that time
Cape Breton Gaels, particularly clergymen, have offered a short
course in the language to any who might be interested.

In addition to the regular day-time class-work there are
evening meetings, which are well attended; on these occasions
Gaelic entertainers and speakers revive their native tongue and
traditions, and to judge from the silent attention and responsive
laughter and appreciative enthusiasm of the audience, the
Gaelic language is far from dead. Wit, oratory, stories, songs,
and pipe-music are the refreshing characteristics of such meetings. The white light of the gasoline pressure lamp shines on the
the alert, weather-tanned faces of the audience in the foreground
and dimly penetrates to the far end of the hall, where the young
lads are leaning against the walls. The massive log walls echo
flatly to the torrent of music that blasts from the bagpipes. The
tune ends, and the wind escapes from the relinquished pouch
with a final skirl through the drones. The speaker of the evening
comes forward and begins his address in the soft tones peculiar
to Gaelic. Roddie Angus leans forward and rests his elbows on
his knees, a half quizzical and expectant attentiveness in his
features, and a merry twinkle in his eye. Red Murdock sits next

him, apparently solemn, and his face expressionless. John A. straightens himself in his seat with the dignity conveyed by white hair and prepares to listen. The words pour from the speaker in an expressive variation of diminuendo and crescendo, one cadent vowel alternating with the next. He reaches the climax of the story; the audience listen as if mesmerized, the trigger of a joke is sprung, and they burst into laughter, a genuine responsive roar of male voices relieved by a higher pitched antiphony from the females. Even the young girls, who might sometimes pretend they do not know much about the language, have been carried away by the speaker and yield to the humour of the ancient tongue.

The scene is one that seems far removed from the twentieth century and from the spruce-clad hills of Nova Scotia; the rich flow of the Gaelic language, the beat of their music, and the distinctively Highland features of the audience belong not to the present but to the distant past when Gaels gathered around a smoky peat fire in some remote island glen, with the drone of the Atlantic surf outside, and the haze of smoke, the fitful light of the fire, and the murmur of happy voices and laughter within.

Now that the speaker of the evening has concluded, the whole assembly join in the chorus of a Gaelic song, composed by Dan Alec MacDonald of Framboise.[15] The leader, a local fisherman, leads off each verse in a firm and melodious tenor voice.

> Bho 'n a tha mi anns an am
> Comhnuidh ann an tir nam beann,
> 'S ged a tha mo Ghaidhlig gann,
> Ni mi rann do thir nan gleannan.

Since I'm now living in the land of the mountains, and although my Gaelic is scanty, I'll put together a verse for the land of glens.

The audience join in deep-throated unison in the chorus:

> 'S e Ceap Breatunn tir mo ghraidh,
> Tir nan craobh 's nam beanntan ard;
> 'S e Ceap Breatunn tir mo ghraidh,
> Tir a's aillidh leinn air thalamh.

Cape Breton is the land of my love, the land of trees and mountains high; Cape Breton is the land of my love, the loveliest land on earth in our opinion.

A minister closes the meeting with a Gaelic prayer; the audience sing "God Save the King" in Gaelic, and then file out into the night. If there are no "little people," no *sithichean*, dancing on the dewy grass, it must surely be because they have been frightened away by the lighting up of bright head-lights and the harsh roar of car engines as the people start off for home!

Attempts such as that of the Gaelic College to preserve the language are rare, and in places where the Gaelic language has decayed, the traditions preserved by the language have also vanished. The old-style Communion Week is not very commonly observed now. Many of the ablest precentors are dead, and the young have not, in general, learned the art from their parents. Not so many Catholic or Protestant clergymen now can preach in Gaelic as could fifty years ago. Folk-tales are nearly forgotten because the old story-tellers are no longer called upon to provide entertainment, and even the Gaelic songs are going out of vogue in favour of card-playing or radio-listening. Milling frolics survive, although often they are only spurious celebrations conducted to raise money for local charities at which a much worn blanket is provided to add legitimacy to the gathering. But were it not for milling frolics and weddings, Gaelic songs would not have survived as well as they have. At both these celebrations there are always a few at least of the older men who are still able to raise a song. The younger people listen and join in the chorus, although they may not be able to understand the less familiar language of the verses.

In spite of these melancholy symptoms of decay, however, much endures that is truly Highland. The wonder is, in fact, that so much has survived. That the language and traditions have been preserved for more than a hundred years and passed down through four, five, and even six generations is a remarkable token of the affection which those of Gaelic blood feel for their heritage.

11

The Rural Life

DURING his first gloomy days in the New World the settler often asked himself whether he had gained anything in crossing the Atlantic and venturing out on a new life of toil and uncertainty. Whatever the original settler may have decided about this question, there is little doubt that his descendants have profited from his enterprise. Those who have chosen to remain in Cape Breton on the farms which the pioneers developed are content to do so because they can now lead a healthy and pleasant life very different from the anxious existence which compelled their ancestors to leave Scotland.

In spite of the diversity among the different Highland settlements in Cape Breton, it is not a difficult task to sketch in general terms the way of life common to all the Gaelic country people. Except for the clergyman, school-teacher, and merchant, the men of the community usually gain their livelihood from one of two possible occupations—farming or fishing. The separation between these two occupations is very slight, since the basis of existence for all of the people is their farm. Some of the men spend the greater part of their time and energy on developing the farming possibilities of their property; others direct their attention more especially to fishing. But the fisherman keeps one or two cows, some hens, a pig, and a horse or two. And although he may do little on the land he at least takes in his hay each year in order to provide winter feed for his live-stock. The full-time farmer has more live-stock than the fisherman and often keeps a small herd of sheep. He raises potatoes and oats and an assortment of vegetables such as carrots, turnips, beets, squash, pumpkin, sweet corn, and lettuce. He may grow apples, plums, and rhubarb, but he does not need to raise much fruit

because it can be found growing wild in great abundance—
strawberries, raspberries, blue-berries, cranberries, and a local
berry (tasting to the uninitiated something like vinegar sweetened
with eau-de-cologne) known as the bake-apple.

The Cape Breton countryman commonly owns between one
and two hundred acres of land, and almost invariably he will tell
you he has more than he needs or wants; if he had less, he would
not have to pay such high taxes. His house is large and of
wooden frame construction. It has a good frost-proof cellar where
supplies are safe in the coldest winter. The heating system is
usually not very elaborate. A certain conservatism prevents him
from installing a furnace. In winter he relies principally on the
heat from the kitchen stove for warmth. The usual fuel is wood
cut from the owner's property; but some who are not able to cut
their own prefer to buy Cape Breton coal and use that instead.
Running water is not common in the houses, but there is an in-
creasing tendency among the people to install plumbing. Most
of the rural districts have not yet been electrified, and kerosene
is the usual source of light. The telephone and the radio, run by
battery, however, are now found in many houses.

In addition to the house proper there is the important out-
building where meat and other supplies are stored in the winter
under ideal refrigerating conditions. There is usually a garage
with a car or a truck in it; and, inevitably, the barn where the
hay is kept and the cattle housed for the long winter and spring
of the year. Besides these buildings the fisherman usually has a
fishing shack and boat-house at the shore.

The seasonal pattern of life is fairly similar, whether a man
specializes in farming or in fishing. The late autumn is a season
of tranquillity. Some fishermen are still busy, but generally the
countryside begins to relax after the labours of the summer. The
farmer, having completed his fall ploughing, takes a vacation
and tramps through the woods in search of deer and partridge.
If he lives near an oyster bed, he may earn some additional
money by raking oysters and shipping them to the city.

In preparation for the cold days ahead both farmer and fisherman bank the outside walls of their houses with eel-grass or
sawdust. When the snow begins to fall the men set out to the

nearest stand of firewood on their property. Quick-kindling soft-wood, particularly spruce, and slow-burning hard-wood, par-ticularly birch, are both necessary. Sometimes the wood has been cut back so far that a search for suitable timber entails a good walk. Then begins the steady work of chopping down trees, trimming them, and piling them ready for hauling home. Those who have the time and energy cut extra wood to be sold for pulp, for pit-props, or for railroad ties. By the time that the wood has been piled, the winter snow has fallen and settled. Horses are then able to haul the wood on skids over a firm path of hard-packed snow to the house, where it is sawed into stove lengths, sometimes by machine, often by hand. The subsequent work of splitting and piling it is performed during leisure moments through the remainder of the winter and the following spring.

Winter is devoted to gaiety, to milling frolics, dances, school concerts, church meetings, Red Cross gatherings, and visiting. Children flock out with their skates on the frozen ponds and lakes and rivers. In some districts horse-and-cutter racing on the ice is still popular. Along the main roads the snow-plough labours through the deep snow, but in the remoter sections trucks and automobiles are stored away for the season, and sleighs are brought out—light riding sleighs for speedy travelling, shining with fresh black and red paint covered with varnish; and sturdy truck sleighs for hauling supplies, roughly constructed with a home-made box and hand-cut shafts. Horses' hooves beat over the hard-packed centre-tracks on the roads; sharp sleigh runners cut into the softer side-tracks; the heavy sleigh bells clang rhythmically. Distant sounds cut through the clear stillness of the atmosphere. All the landscape is covered with snow; the fence posts and the young spruce trees at the edge of the road wear a white cap. From the chimney of each farm-house fragrant wood smoke rises swiftly, and at night yellow lamp-light gleams from the windows.

The joys of winter begin to fade as the cold season drags on into spring—the most generally disliked period of the entire year. When once the crisp snow turns to slush and ice, there is no further pleasure in cold weather. The bards who have sung the praises of Cape Breton are sensitive about this weak point in the attractions of their beloved island, and each apologizes in his own way. Jonathan G. MacKinnon tries to misdirect our attention away from the winter and spring to the beauties of the summer:

> Faodaidh gu'm bi 'n geamhradh fuar
> 'S gaoth an earraich o'n taobh tuath;
> Thig an samhradh blath 'n a uair
> Le cur us buain 'g ar toileachadh.[1]

It may be that the winter is cold, and the wind of spring from the north; warm summer will come in season with sowing and reaping to make us happy.

John V. MacNeil points out that the winter, although cold, does not affect the good nature of the inhabitants:

> Siud an tir 's an biodh an uaill
> Eadar froilicean us luaidh,
> 'S ged a bhiodh an geamhradh fuar,
> Cha bhiodh gruaman air na balaich.
>
> Maighdeannan bu ghrinne beus,
> Thogadh fonn gu pongail, reidh;
> Nuair a shuidheadh iad aig cleith
> Co nach eisdeadh ri 'n ceol-aighir?[2]

That's the land where there's gaiety, what with frolics and millings, and although the winter's cold, the boys aren't grumpy.

Girls of the kindest courtesy will raise a melody true and even; when they sit at the milling-board, who wouldn't listen to their happy song?

The most elaborate apology for the cold comes from N. K. Mac-Leod, who explains—perhaps not very poetically—that it is all the fault of the drift-ice which piles up on the shores of Cape Breton in the winter:

> Mur biodh an deigh-dhriftidh bhith tighinn o'n tuath
> 'S a' Mhart us 's a' Ghiblin le fliuchadh us fuachd,
> Bhiodh blathas anna a' Mhart anns gach aite mu'n cuairt;
> Bhiodh duileach air coille anns gach doire agus bruach.[3]

If the drift-ice weren't coming from the north in March and April with wet and cold, there would be warmth in March in every place around, there would be leafage on the trees over every grove and hill-side.

The poet even goes so far as to propose an ingenious remedy, which seems however to have been ignored by the provincial authorities:

> Na'm biodh Caolas Belle Isle, naoidh mile tarsuing,
> Duinte le torr ro mhor de chlachan,
> Bhiodh blathas anns a' Mhart 's gach aite deas air;
> Bhiodh deigh Baffin's Bay gun bheud dol seachad.

> If the Strait of Belle Isle, nine miles across, were closed with an enormous pile of stones, there would be warmth in March everywhere south of it; the ice of Baffin's Bay would go past without harm.

The spring, although unpleasant, has its compensations. Tasty smelt can be caught in inlets and rivers by fishing through holes cut in the ice, and when it melts they can be scooped up by the hundreds as they swarm up the brooks. Succulent eels can be speared in the mud. The caplin race into the brooks. The gaspereaux (known elsewhere as alewives) swim up the swift-running rivers in stupid determination right into the net.

As the spring moves grudgingly along there is always plenty of work for the men-folk to do. The farmer gets his equipment ready for planting. The fisherman overhauls his boat and engine, and mends his nets, or completes his lobster traps. Both fisherman and farmer inspect their fences and put in new posts and poles wherever they are needed. The cows calve; the mares foal; the sheep lamb; the hens are set on their eggs, and hatch out their chicks, and the household cat proudly summons her new kittens out from the barn.

Then the busy season begins. The fisherman leaves his house and takes up his residence at the shore, immersing himself in a tangle of rope, lines, crates, kegs, barrels, nets, traps, hooks, and buckets. In a short time he is out to sea, setting the traps and nets, trying to guess where the fish will run this season. From then on through the summer he is never idle. Each kind of fish requires special gear and a special technique—salmon, herring, mackerel, cod, lobster—and all require incessant watchfulness and toil.

The farmer, at the same time, is trying to foresee what nature is going to bring him in the way of weather. He begins to plough and harrow and sow and plant. Summer moves on. The seeds entrusted to the soil thrust out green blades. Finally the season for the harvest arrives. After a bustle of activity the harvest is brought home. The tempo of life slows down. The people are secure for another year. Whatever may befall, they will have plenty to eat.

The women-folk on the farms are busy at all seasons, and their work does not present the same seasonal variety as the men's. Their principal jobs are cooking and cleaning and raising children. They remain indoors very largely and take less share in the outside work than their mothers did. Eighty, or even fifty, years ago the women had to work out in the fields as hard as any man; they might be expected to split their own fire-wood once it had been sawed for them; they would certainly be expected to milk the cows. Now they do not usually work outside except at haying time; and if a man dared to leave them without any fire-wood split, he would hear about his neglect later in no uncertain terms. Nor do they milk the cows if they can find an unoccupied man to perform the chore. Even although at home they have been required to do the milking daily, girls who hire out to help on farms try to evade this part of the work by pretending that they are frightened of cows. The emancipation of women in the New World has gained them more than the power to vote—a great deal more, the men-folk say.

In the Highlands and Islands of Scotland a traveller might journey far before he would come upon an inn, but the country people were always willing and proud to offer food, shelter, and hospitality to friend or stranger without thought of return. One of the Statutes of Icolumkill, drawn up in 1609 for the purpose of reforming the state of the Highlands and Western Islands, required that inns should be established in the country in order to save the substance of over-generous people who squandered their means on this free-handed type of entertaining.[4] But, whatever the immediate effects of the legislation, the ancient tradition survives among the Highland people in the New World, and it is the woman of the house who dispenses this hospitality to the wanderer and the guest. As soon as a visitor appears, even though he may be only an Indian selling baskets, or a Syrian peddler, the housewife moves the kettle over the hot part of the stove to boil and warms the teapot. If the visitor arrives after the regular meal-time he is given a "lunch"; if he arrives, either unintentionally or intentionally, just before meal-time an extra place is set for him at the kitchen table. A visitor is automatically accepted just like another member of the family and fed. If he is travelling far, his horse is stabled or his car put under shelter, and a bed is prepared for him. When bed-time comes, he is given a lamp and shown to his room. No one could treat a guest with kindliness more sincere or with attention more unostentatious than even the humblest Gael bestows on the traveller. It is a sad and unvisited home where the housewife fails in this duty.

Cookery—the woman's art—has undergone a great change since first the Highland women set up homes on these shores. The traditional diet of the Highlander in Scotland at the time of the emigrations is said to have consisted of fish and boiled potatoes. In the New World the immigrants amplified this diet considerably, although it is still limited by the refrigerating problem. In the heat of summer, fish, cured or freshly caught, is still the mainstay; but in the winter, when provisions can be preserved by freezing, meat makes its appearance. The repertoire of the menu has been enlarged, moreover, by the increased quantity of fruit and vegetables once unknown in the Highlands which are now available in the New World. Some traditional Highland dishes remain to lend individuality to the Gael's table, such as porridge and oat bread. Others have unaccountably become very rare, such as the meat sausage known as *iosban*, or the oatmeal sausage known as *marag gheal*, or the blood sausage known as *marag dhubh*. The art of preparing home-made cheese is almost forgotten; although, in a few exceptional districts such as Mabou, sufficient quantities of a firm, whitish cheese are produced by home manufacture to sell in the local stores.

The average family lives very well. In winter when it is impossible to get to a store the wise farmer or fisherman has a well-stocked house. Even in an isolated settlement at this time of the year it is not uncommon to find in a fisherman's house fresh eggs, milk, cream, and butter; half a carcass of beef hanging frozen in the out-house; a barrelful of home-killed pork, and cuts of home-cured ham and bacon; a hundred-pound box of dry-salt-cod, a barrel of salt herring; miscellaneous frozen fish recently caught, such as cod, skate, and eels; home-canned salmon and lobster; a cellarful of vegetables and home-canned fruit; and a store of other necessities purchased in the autumn.

Frequently we find in Cape Breton that neither the farmer nor the fisherman is a specialist in any one branch of his calling. Primarily he tries to raise enough food by his own exertions that he may be self-supporting. Whatever extra he sells provides him with cash. He may add to his income during quiet seasons by working part-time on highway construction and maintenance or on the railroad, or by keeping a post office or store. The "people away" often send generous contributions back home to keep their old homestead going. The countryman's financial needs are not great, although every year sees them increase.

Many country people, however, are losing faith in their way of life. Listen to any intelligent farmer or fisherman in conversation:

"You can't get enough out of farming now. It used to be all right when we didn't need much, but now there's expensive machinery to buy, and there are taxes to pay, and they keep going up each year, and the women like to get some new clothes now and again."

"I don't blame the young fellows for going off to the cities where they can get easy money. This is a tough country, all rocks and spruce trees. The soil is ruined; it's turned sour with overworking. It's nice here in the summer, but the winter's hard. It costs so much to get through the cold season. There's no money coming in, and you're using up your own stuff all the time—food, fire-wood, hay—and you don't get anything in return for it."

"Farming would be all right if you knew what the prices were going to be. Last year I had a little plot of turnips, and they turned out to be worth their weight in gold; the towns just gobbled them up. So this year I put in a whole field of them, and now I can't give them away. The towns are yellow with turnips."

"I could raise all kinds of stuff on this farm, but what's the use of that? It would cost me so much to send the stuff to a market that I'd make no profit on it, or else I couldn't find any market for it at all."

"Fishing is all right, but it's a tough life. You're out in all kinds of weather and you work all day and half the night. And you never know when you're going to make money. You have to keep a lot of expensive gear in good running order because you can't catch fish without it, and then when fish are scarce you can't even cover expenses. Of course, the price goes up these times—it may go up so high that it's a scandal, and no ordinary person can afford to buy your fish; but still the fisherman doesn't make anything out of it. Then the next season fish will be plenty, but the price will go down so low that it's not worth your while to go on catching the things, and all you get is a back-ache. And when the price is just right, a storm will come along and take away all your gear, and you don't get any fish, or any money either."

The faith of the countryman is pinned no longer on fishing and farming but on industry. In his mind the solution to the plight of Cape Breton is to encourage bigger and better industries. Malcolm Gillis tells us as much in one of his songs in praise of his native island:

> Ma bhios luchd-riaghlaidh na duthcha fialaidh
> Cha bhi ar n-iargain dol fad thar chuimhn',
> Gu'm bi 'n t-each-iaruinn tigh'nn troimh na criochan
> Le uprait fhiadhaich air feadh gach tuim
> Bheir faisg oirnn margadh 's a sgapas airgead
> Air feadh nan garbh chrioch; 's le foirm thar tuinn
> Gu'n till na cairdean a rinn ar fagail,
> 'S gu'n dean sinn abhachd 'nuair theid sinn cruinn.
>
> Bidh meinean luachmhor an sin 'g am fuasgladh,
> Bidh beairteas buan duinn an tir mo ghraidh;
> Chan fhaicear smuairean air neach a ghlauiseas
> Air feadh nam bruachan as uaine blath;
> Bidh solas inntinn gu pailt ag cinntinn,
> 'S gu linn nan linntean chan fhaic sinn sas
> An Tir nam Beanntan, an gaol tha teann duinn
> O'm faighear neoinean 's a' ghleann a' fas.[5]

If the leaders of the country will be bountiful, they will not for long overlook our concern that there should be a railway through the districts coming with wild uproar past each hillock in order to bring a market near to us and to spread money among the country places;

and our people who left us will return proudly from over the waves, and we'll celebrate when we gather together.

Valuable mines will be opened then; we'll have enduring wealth in the land of my love; there will be no worries for anyone who stirs among the hill-sides of greenest herbage; contentment will grow abundantly, and to the age of ages we shall not see distress in the Land of the Mountains, which we have loved so strongly since we picked the daisies growing in the glen.

What the leaders of the country will actually do with rural Cape Breton is an interesting problem. Governmental and educational agencies are at present trying to help the people to profit from the obvious resources of the country—its farm products and fish—without relying on industry. The schools are trying to interest students in making the most out of the potentialities around them and to offer to country children opportunities for education as rich as they could find in any city. The agricultural and the fisheries departments of the government are trying to introduce more convenient and suitable methods of work and of marketing. The adult education department of St. Francis Xavier University is encouraging rural libraries and training the country people in the methods of the co-operative movement, whereby they may finance their own undertakings more economically and produce more by their own labour. Health authorities are enlarging their rural facilities, so that women need have no dread of child-birth in remote country districts; so that accidents can be attended to quickly; and so that disease may be promptly isolated and eradicated. Perhaps the most important consideration for the future is the intangible but real fact that the people themselves enjoy their country life. They may complain of hardships and poverty, but they love the beauties of their surroundings; they live a tranquil life, secure in the knowledge that they will never starve or be unemployed, as their city cousins may be; they enjoy good health and are able to raise their children in a clean environment. They envy the city dwellers their conveniences, amusements, and luxuries, but they are glad to avoid the noise, smoke, dust, dirt, congestion, and frenzy of the city.

By a process of natural selection those who have chosen to remain in Cape Breton and make their living by fishing have

done so because they feel an inborn attraction to the sea. As Red
Dan said, "I once went to Boston and got a job as a carpenter.
The work was easy enough, and I was getting all the money I
needed, but I got tired of it all. I quit after a few weeks and
headed right for the wharves to get a job on the first fishing boat
that needed a man. It's beside the sea that I was born, and I've
spent all my time on it from the first day that I was allowed to
go out in a row boat. I'd never be satisfied anywhere else."

Similarly, the farmer who has remained on the soil has done
so because it satisfies him to watch the rise and fall of his horses'
muscles as they pull on the traces of the plough, and to feel the
clean cut of the ploughshare through firm sod. He might, quite
possibly, be loath to confess that he harboured such feelings,
but his songs avouch the emotions otherwise unvoiced. Gaelic
nature poetry, whether composed in Scotland or in Cape Breton,
expresses more than a parochial pride in the local scene. Duncan
Ban MacIntyre is, of course, convinced that no mountain could
be more splendid than Ben Dorain, but his primary concern is
to express the satisfaction which it has so abundantly afforded
him. Donald MacDonald claims that the rear of Margaree is
more charming than the shore, but the real theme of his song
is the kindred satisfaction which he also has achieved in his
environment. In the *Song of MacDonald's Mountain*,[6] Angus
R. MacDonald has ingeniously succeeded in epitomizing his
countrymen's latent appreciation of nature by allowing the
Mountain itself to speak to man.

> Bha mi an seo mu'n d' thainig Criosda,
> 'S mi 'nam laidhe 'n seo air m' fhiaradh
> Leis an lochan seo ri m' chliathaich;
> Do Chloinn Domhnuill chaidh ar deanamh.
>
> 'S iomadh feum a rinn mi riamh dhuibh,
> Ged nach d' fhuair mi taing no fiach air—
> Cumail connaidh agus biadh ribh
> Anns gach doigh a rinn sibh iarraidh.
>
> Bidh eallach air mo dhruim 's an t-samhradh
> De chrodh-laoigh, de dh' eich, 's de ghamhna;
> 'S mi 'g an arach dhuibh o Bhealltuinn
> Gus an tig am fuachd 's a' gheamhradh.

Thug mi dhuibh gu leor de choirce
'S de bhuntata mar a chosg sibh,
Fiar le dias bu bhreagha spealta,
'S dearcagan us clobhar am pailteas.

Tha lochan beag an seo 'nam achlais,
Bric us easgannan ro phailt ann.
Am feasgar ciuin le driuchd gu'm faic sibh
Cuartagan mu'n cuairt a' sgapadh.

Fhad 's a bhios na neoil a' gluasad
Mar a chuireas 'ghaoth mu'n cuairt iad,
Fanaidh mise an seo gun ghluasad
Ri Cloinn Domhnuill fhad 's is buan iad.

I was here before Christ came, lying down with this little lake at my side; for the MacDonalds we were created.

Many a bounty have I ever supplied you although I received neither thanks nor recognition for it—providing fire-wood and food for you in every form that you desired.

Every summer on my back there is a burden of milk-cows, horses, and heifers, and I rear them for you from May-day until the cold of winter comes.

I provided you oats in plenty and potatoes as you needed them, hay with the handsomest head ever mowed, berries and clover in abundance.

In the crook of my arm I hold a little lake, in which trout and eels abound; on a calm evening at dew-fall you will see round ripples widening over it.

As long as the clouds are drifting whatever way the wind may blow them, I shall remain here unmoving for the MacDonalds while they endure.

The substance of Gaelic nature poetry, is, to be sure, conventional; but the feelings expressed are not, therefore, necessarily feigned. The satisfaction afforded by nature to the settlers' descendants, traditional though its expression may be, is as genuine as any other attitude inherited from their forefathers and willingly embraced. Although they may deprecatingly reply to the visitor who admires the scenery of Cape Breton, "Well, yes, it's all right in the summer," yet they actually love the lakes and inlets, the abrupt hill-sides and long valleys of their island home. The problem which the future must solve is to find a method by which the financial reward of the farmer's and fisherman's labours may equal the inner satisfaction which they have achieved.

Notes

~~~~~~

ALL QUOTATIONS, English and Gaelic, in this book have been faithfully reproduced word for word. Spelling and punctuation in both languages, however, have been somewhat standardized. There are three difficulties facing those who publish Gaelic material.

First, an independent spirit among writers of Gaelic and particularly among printers of the language emboldens them to ignore all the nice proprieties of Gaelic orthography and to mis-spell words with great abandon. These mis-spellings I have tried to correct.

Secondly, there is no accepted standard method of spelling some words. *So* meaning "here," *sud* meaning "there," *is* meaning "and," and *tigh* meaning "house" are the traditional methods of spelling these words; but since these spellings in each case violate the customary phonetic significance of certain combinations of letters, reformers spell these words *seo*, *siud*, *us*, and *taigh*. I have adapted all quotations to this reformed convention out of a personal preference for consistency over traditionalism. Other variations in spelling are not so easily evaluated, such as *cha'n eil*, *chan eil*, and *cha n-eil*, or *fa leith*, *fa leath*, *fa leth*, and the like. I have tried in general to bring such variations into accord with the standard set by Edward Dwelly's *Illustrated Gaelic-English Dictionary* (4th ed., Glasgow, 1941).

Thirdly, variations in orthography sometimes indicate phonetically the difference between one dialect of Gaelic and another and actually aid the reader in recreating the sound value given to a word by the writer. Such variations add life to Gaelic, however confusing they may be to the uninitiated, and in the case of poetry are sometimes vital to a successful understanding of the assonance of a verse. The most commonly occurring fluctuation is between the sound represented by *eu* and the sound represented by *ia*, such as in *ceud* and *ciad*, meaning "hundred." I have retained these variations.

The translations appended to all Gaelic quotations were made by my wife and myself. We have attempted to convey the emotional and poetic meaning of the Gaelic by using idiomatic English rather than a severely literal translation, word for word, and twist for twist. The latter method might, it is true, make the reader suspect that he was tasting something of the quaint flavour of the original; but it would seriously misrepresent the succinct and expressive idiom peculiar to the Gaelic language.

In the notes the works are referred to in full, the author, title, and place and date of publication each being specified when known, except in the case of several works which are mentioned so frequently that for the sake of convenience they are quoted by a short title; below is a detailed list of these abbreviated references.

SHORT TITLES

Caraid: Caraid nan Gaidheal, Gaelic Writings by Norman MacLeod [of St. Columba's], selected and edited by the Reverend A. Clerk. Edinburgh, 1910.

Carmichael, *Carmina:* Alexander Carmichael, *Carmina Gadelica*, Edinburgh; vols. 1-2, 1900; vol. 3, 1940; vol. 4, 1941.

Casket: The Casket, a weekly paper, Antigonish, N.S.; vol. 1, no. 1, published in June 24, 1852; still current.

Centenary: Centenary of the First Landing of a Catholic Bishop on the Shores of the Bras d'Or Lakes, Cape Breton, 1815-1915. N.p., n.d.

Clarsach: Clarsach na Coille, ed. by the Reverend Alexander Maclean Sinclair; revised by Hector MacDougall. Glasgow, 1928.

Clippings: Five volumes of articles on Gaelic culture, clipped from newspapers by the Reverend Alexander Maclean Sinclair (usually without indication of source). Now in possession of his son, George Maclean Sinclair, Hopewell, N.S.

Fear: Fear na Ceilidh, a Gaelic monthly, Sydney, N.S. [ed. by Jonathan G. Mac-Kinnon]; vol. 1, no. 1, published March, 1928. Not continued after the conclusion of vol. 2.

Gaelic Bards: The Gaelic Bards from 1825 to 1875, ed. by the Reverend Alexander Maclean Sinclair. Sydney, N.S., 1904.

Gaidheal: An Gaidheal, a Gaelic magazine, ed. by Angus Nicholson. First number published Toronto, 1871; subsequently published in Glasgow.

Hutchinson, *Directory:* Thomas Hutchinson, *Nova Scotia Directory for 1864-1865.* Halifax, N.S., n.d.

Johnson, *Journey:* Samuel Johnson, *A Journey to the Western Islands of Scotland* in *The Works of Samuel Johnson* (London, 1816), vol. 8, pp. 205-412.

MacDougall, *History:* John L. MacDougall, *History of Inverness County, Nova Scotia.* N.p., n.d.; preface dated at Strathlorne, N.S., 1922.

MacKenzie, *History:* Archibald J. MacKenzie, *History of Christmas Island Parish.* N.p., n.d.; preface dated 1926.

MacLean, *Typographia:* Reverend Donald MacLean, *Typographia Scoto-Gadelica.* Edinburgh, 1915.

MacLeod, *Reminiscences:* Reverend Norman MacLeod [of the Barony], *Reminiscences of a Highland Parish.* 2nd ed., London, 1833.

Mac-Talla: Mac-Talla, ed. by Jonathan G. MacKinnon, Sydney, N.S. A Gaelic newspaper, published weekly beginning with vol. 1, no. 1 (May 28, 1892), until vol. 10, no. 16; thereafter published every two weeks until terminated in vol. 12, no. 26 (June 24, 1904).

Martell, *Immigration:* James S. Martell, *Immigration to and Emigration from Nova Scotia, 1815-1838.* Public Archives of N.S., Publication no. 6. Halifax, N.S., 1942.

Morrison, *Orain:* Murdoch Morrison, *Orain Fuinn is Cladaich.* Glasgow, 1931.

Murray, *History:* Reverend John Murray, *The History of the Presbyterian Church in Cape Breton.* Truro, N.S., 1921.

Patterson, *Memoir:* Reverend George Patterson, *Memoir of the Rev. James Mac-Gregor.* Philadelphia, 1859.

Smeorach: Smeorach nan Cnoc 's nan Gleann, compiled by Bernard Gillis and the Reverend Dr. P. J. Nicholson, ed. by Hector MacDougall. Glasgow, 1939.

Teachdaire nan Gaidheal: Teachdaire nan Gaidheal (Gaelic Herald), a Gaelic periodical ed. by James MacNeil, assisted by the Reverend Norman MacDonald. Sydney, N.S.

Preface (pp. vii-ix)

1. See John Patterson MacLean, *An Historical Account of the Settlements of Scotch Highlanders in America* (Cleveland, Ohio, and Glasgow, 1900); Martell, *Immigration;* Mrs. R. G. Flewwelling, "Immigration to and Emigration from Nova Scotia, 1839-1851," *Collections of the Nova Scotia Historical Society,* vol. 28 (1949), pp. 75-105. Daniel C. Harvey gives a convenient summary of the immigrants to the Canadian Maritimes in two articles: "Early Settlement in Prince Edward Island," *Dalhousie Review,* vol. 11 (Jan., 1932), pp. 448 ff., and "Scotch Immigration to Cape Breton," *ibid.,* vol. 21 (Oct., 1941), pp. 313 ff. Edwin C. Guillet gives a concise account of the Glengarry County Highlanders in his *Early Life in Upper Canada* (Toronto, 1933), pp. 35 ff. There are several other Highland settlements in Canada which have not been mentioned in the present work because of the scarcity of

information about them. There is, for instance, the group in Megantic County, Quebec, mentioned by W. M. MacKenzie in *The Book of Arran* (Glasgow, 1914), vol. 2, pp. 218 ff.

2. Charles W. Dunn, "Check-List of Scottish Gaelic Writings in North America," *Irisleabhar Ceilteach*, vol. 1 (Toronto, 1952), pp. 23-9.

3. *Eighth Census of Canada, 1941*, Population: no. A-9 (Nova Scotia).

Chapter 1 (pp. 3-10)

1. The early history of the Gaels or Goidels is shrouded in obscurity. See Henri Hubert, *The Rise of the Celts*, trans. from the French by M. R. Dobie (London, 1934), pp. 188 ff., and, by the same author and translator, *The Greatness and Decline of the Celts* (London, 1934), pp. 158 ff.; also a brief account in Eoin MacNeill, *Phases of Irish History* (Dublin, 1920), pp. 194-221. Even at a period as remote as the settlement of Scotland the ancestors of the present Gaelic-speaking population were of mixed origin.

2. William Forbes Skene in *The Highlanders of Scotland* (2nd ed., Stirling, 1902), pp. 1-157, traces the national development of the Highlanders in Scotland.

3. See James A. H. Murray, "The Dialect of the Southern Counties of Scotland," *Transactions of the Philological Society, 1870-1872*, pt. II (London, 1873), pp. 1-19, for a summary of the formation of the Lowland group.

4. V. Gordon Childe, *The Prehistory of Scotland* (London, 1935), pp. 259-67. See also H. M. Chadwick, *Early Scotland: The Picts, the Scots, and the Welsh of Southern Scotland* (Cambridge, 1949).

5. See George Henderson, *The Norse Influence on Celtic Scotland* (Glasgow, 1910), especially pp. 1-39.

6. See Cosmo Innes, *Scotland in the Middle Ages* (Edinburgh, 1860), pp. 88-9.

7. Bartholomaeus Anglicus, *Liber de proprietatibus rerum* (Strassburg, 1491), bk. 15, ch. 152. The translation of *silvestres* as "wild" occurs in John Trevisa's fourteenth-century English selections from Bartholomew reprinted in *Medieval Lore from Bartholomew Anglicus* by Robert Steele (London, 1924), p. 99.

8. John Major, *Historia Maioris Britanniae* (Edinburgh, 1740), p. 33 (bk. 1, ch. 8).

9. K. H. Huggins, "The Scottish Highlands: A Regional Study," *Scottish Geographical Magazine*, vol. 51 (1935), pp. 296 ff.

10. *Scotland* (The Blue Guides), ed. by Findlay Muirhead (London and Paris, 1927), contains such geographical information in convenient form.

11. Johnson, *Journey*, p. 313.

12. Alexander Stevens, "The Human Geography of Lewis," *Scottish Geographical Magazine*, vol. 41 (1925), pp. 75-88.

13. Daniel Defoe, *A Tour thro' the Island of Great Britain*, ed. by G. D. H. Cole (London, 1927), vol. 2, p. 831.

14. Both may be found, along with an English translation, in *The Gaelic Songs of Duncan MacIntyre*, ed. with translation by George Calder (Edinburgh, 1912), pp. 160-97, 406-13.

15. From his *Iorram Cuain*, which may be found, along with an English translation, in *The Poems of Alexander MacDonald*, ed. with translation by the Reverend A. MacDonald of Killearnan and the Reverend A. MacDonald of Kiltarlity (Inverness, 1924), pp. 364-9.

16. From *Moladh na Luinge* in *Sar-Obair nam Bard Gaelach: The Beauties of Gaelic Poetry*, ed. by John MacKenzie (Edinburgh, 1907), pp. 295-6.

17. Donald MacKechnie, *Am Fear-Ciuil* (2nd ed., Edinburgh, 1910), p. 9.

Chapter 2 (pp. 11-23)

1. Johnson, *Journey*, p. 273.

2. Isabel Frances Grant, *The Social and Economic Development of Scotland before 1603* (Edinburgh, 1930), pp. 506-7.

3. Johnson, *Journey*, p. 275.

4. Of the many discussions concerning the reasons for the Highland emigration, the following seem outstanding: three articles by M. I. Adam in the *Scottish Historical Review*, "The Highland Emigration of 1770," vol. 16, no. 64 (July, 1919), pp. 281-93,

"The Causes of the Highland Emigrations, 1783-1803," vol. 17, no. 66 (Jan., 1920), pp. 73-89, "Eighteenth Century Landlords and the Poverty Problem," vol. 19, no. 73 (Oct., 1921), pp. 1-20, and no. 75 (April, 1922), pp. 161-79; Isabel Frances Grant, *Every-day Life on an Old Highland Farm, 1769-1782* (London, 1924), pp. 35-6; Isabel Frances Grant, *The Economic History of Scotland* (London, 1934), pp. 212-14, 229; D. F. MacDonald, *Scotland's Shifting Population*, 1770-1850 (Glasgow, 1937), pp. 43-4, 140-9.

5. By an anonymous author in *Blackwood's Edinburgh Magazine* (Sept., 1829). See G. H. Needler, *The Lone Shieling* (Toronto, 1941).

6. Allan R. MacDonald, *The Truth about Flora MacDonald*, ed. by D. MacKinnon (Inverness, 1939), pp. 85-91.

7. Donald Gregory, *The History of the Western Highlands and Isles of Scotland from 1493 to 1625* (2nd ed., London, 1881), p. 416.

8. See Alphons Bellesheim, *History of the Catholic Church of Scotland*, trans. by D. O. H. Blair (1890), vol. 4, pp. 163 ff.

9. The late Reverend Donald M. MacAdam, then parish priest at Sydney; see *The Canadian-American Gael*, vol. 1 (Cape Breton Island ed., Sydney, N.S., 1943), p. 87.

10. *Centenary*, pp. 14, 16.

11. Robert Brown, *Strictures and Remarks on the Earl of Selkirk's Observations on the Present State of the Highlands of Scotland* (1806), quoted in M. I. Adam, "The Causes of the Highland Emigrations, 1783-1803," *Scottish Historical Review*, vol. 17, no. 66 (Jan., 1920), p. 78.

12. David Stewart, *Sketches of the Character of the Highlanders of Scotland* (2nd ed., Edinburgh, 1822), vol. 1, p. 131.

13. MacKenzie, *History*, pp. 99-100.

14. Alasdair Friseal [= Alexander Fraser], *Leabhar nan Sonn* (Toronto, 1897), pp. 68, 73. See also *The Encyclopedia of Canada*, ed. by W. S. Wallace (Toronto, 1936), under "Archibald McKellar."

15. *Holland's Description of Cape Breton Island and other Documents*, compiled by Daniel C. Harvey, Public Archives of Nova Scotia, Publication no. 2 (Halifax, 1935), p. 122.

16. *Teachdaire Gaelach*, Glasgow, 1829-31; *Teachdaire Ur Gaelach*, Glasgow, 1835-6; and *Cuairtear nan Gleann*, Glasgow, 1840-3.

17. There are three ministers by the name of Norman MacLeod mentioned in the present work: (1) the Reverend Doctor Norman MacLeod, 1783-1862, minister of St. Columba's Chapel, Glasgow, a distinguished Gaelic writer; (2) his son, the Reverend Doctor Norman MacLeod, 1812-1872, minister of the Barony, Glasgow; (3) the Reverend Norman McLeod, 1780-1866, minister of St. Ann's, Cape Breton Island, N.S., who subsequently led his followers to New Zealand. Concerning the first two see Hew Scott, *Fasti Ecclesiae Scoticanae* (new ed., Edinburgh, 1920), vol. 3, pp. 121, 377, 394, 437; concerning the third see Murray, *History*, pp. 20-34, 71-4. Whenever mentioned here each is identified by the name of his congregation.

18. I have not seen a copy of the *Ceann-Iuil*, but a review of it appears in *Cuairtear nan Gleann*, Sept., 1841, p. 205.

19. Martell, *Immigration*, pp. 10, 36. Further mention of MacNiven's activities may be found in *Mac-Talla*, vol. 2, no. 49, p. 2; in *The Book of Barra*, ed. by John Lorne Campbell (London, 1936), p. 180; and in *The MacDonald Collection of Gaelic Poetry*, ed. by the Reverend A. MacDonald of Killearnan and the Reverend A. MacDonald of Kiltarlity (Inverness, 1911), p. 370.

20. *Clarsach*, pp. 90-4.

21. Martell, *Immigration*, pp. 12, 27-8.

22. *Ibid.*, p. 59.

23. MacKenzie, *History*, p. 20.

24. D. F. MacDonald, *Scotland's Shifting Population, 1770-1850* (Glasgow, 1937), p. 144.

25. Martell, *Immigration*, p. 60.

26. *Ibid.*, pp. 37-9.

27. MacDougall, *History*, pp. 126-31.

28. Martell, *Immigration*, p. 49.

29. John Sealgair MacDonald, *Oran do dh' America*, as recorded in *Gaelic Bards*, pp. 40-3. A more complete version appears in *Casket*, Aug. 21, 1930, p. 8.

30. In *Caraid*, pp. 263-73. An English translation by the Reverend Archibald Clerk may be found in MacLeod, *Reminiscences*, pp. 378-92.

Chapter 3 (pp. 24-33)

1. Crawley in a letter to Sir Rupert D. George dated May 28, 1827, at Sydney, N.S., preserved at the Public Archives of Nova Scotia, Halifax, in volume 335, document 112. Quoted in Martell, *Immigration*, p. 14.

2. Crawley in another letter to George dated June 11, 1827, at Sydney, at same source as specified in note 1. Quoted in Martell, *Immigration*, p. 22.

3. In R. C. MacDonald, *Sketches of Highlanders* (St. John, N.B., 1843), "Appendix," p. ii.

4. MacKenzie, *History*, pp. 4, 120.

5. Quoted in Jonathan G. MacKinnon, *Old Sydney: Sketches of the Town and Its People in Days Gone By* (Sydney, N.S., 1918), pp. 90-1. Various informants in the Mira district of Cape Breton identified the author, whose name is not specified by MacKinnon.

6. The Reverend Roderick MacKenzie, "The Early Missions on the Bras d'Or Lakes," in *Centenary*, and quoted in MacKenzie, *History*, pp. 3-4.

7. Michael D. Currie, "Pioneer Days in Cape Breton," in *Teachdaire nan Gaidheal*, vol. 5, no. 2 (Christmas, 1932), p. 11.

8. John MacRae, *Duanag Altruim*, in *The Gaelic Bards from 1715 to 1765*, ed. by the Reverend Alexander Maclean Sinclair (Charlottetown, P.E.I., 1892), p. 258.

9. In *Oran do dh' America; Clarsach*, pp. 90-4.

10. *Ibid.*

11. See, for instance, the account of the settler's life in Upper Canada given by an anonymous Gaelic writer in *Cuairtear nan Gleann*, later republished in *Rosg Gaidhlig: Specimens of Gaelic Prose*, ed. by William J. Watson (2nd ed., Glasgow, 1929), pp. 102-7. Lauchlan Currie composed an amusing song, *Oran an Teine*, about a fire that went out of hand; it is published in *Fear*, vol. 1, no. 7 (Sept., 1928), p. 54, and in the *Casket*, July 4, 1935, p. 8.

12. There is an illustration and description of this instrument in Edward Dwelly, *The Illustrated Gaelic-English Dictionary* (4th ed., Glasgow, 1941), p. 172.

13. C. H. D. Clarke, *Investigation of Cape Breton Highlands National Park*, March 23, 1942 (mimeographed pamphlet issued by the Department of Mines and Resources, Canada), p. 5.

14. Judge George Patterson, *The History of Victoria County*, a manuscript written for the Akins Historical Prize, 1885, in King's College Library, Halifax, N.S.

15. *Letters of Rev. Norman McLeod* [of St. Ann's], *1835-1851*, ed. by Daniel C. Harvey, Bulletin of the Public Archives of Nova Scotia, vol. 2, no. 1 (Halifax, 1939), p. 22.

16. MacKenzie, *History*, p. 105.

17. The jacket is in the possession of William MacVicar, Catalone, Cape Breton; it was made for his brother.

18. In *Oran do dh' America; Clarsach*, pp. 90-4.

19. *The Arrival of the First Scottish Catholic Emigrants in Prince Edward Island and after: Memorial Volume, 1772-1922*, published by a committee on the occasion of the erection of a monument at Scotchfort (Summerside, P.E.I., 1922), pp. 30-1.

20. In his report on Common Pleas for the Upper District of Sydney County, dated February 16, 1828, at Truro, N.S., preserved at the Public Archives of Nova Scotia, Halifax, in volume 235, document 8. I am indebted for this and several other references to the late J. S. Martell, Assistant Archivist.

21. "Eastern Rambles," no. 7, in his weekly newspaper, the *Novascotian*, July 1, 1830, p. 206.

Chapter 4 (pp. 34-57)

1. Narrated in an autobiographical sketch quoted by his son, Norman MacLeod of the Barony, in *Caraid*, "Biographical Sketch of the Author," p. xxi.

2. The first Scottish Gaelic translation of the entire Bible was begun in 1786 but not completed until 1801. See the Reverend Donald MacKinnon, *The Gaelic Bible and Psalter* (Dingwall, 1930), pp. 59-61.

3. See MacKinnon's book mentioned in note 2, pp. 47, 54-6.

4. James Boswell, *Journal of a Tour of the Hebrides with Samuel Johnson, Now First Published from the Original Manuscript in the Isham Collection* (New York and London, 1936), Oct. 29, 1773, p. 364.

5. Johnson's "Letter to William Drummond," Aug. 13, 1766, in James Boswell, *The Life of Samuel Johnson*, ed. by Roger Ingpen (Bath, 1925), vol. 1, pp. 316, 318.

6. See Edward G. Cox, "The Case of Scotland *vs.* Dr. Samuel Johnson," *Transactions of the Gaelic Society of Inverness*, vol. 32 (1925-7), pp. 49-79, and Charles W. Dunn, "Highland Song and Lowland Ballad," *University of Toronto Quarterly*, vol. 18 (1948), pp. 1-19.

7. *The Register of the Privy Council of Scotland*, ed. by David Masson (Edinburgh, 1891), vol. 10, p. 671.

8. Sheriff MacMaster Campbell, "The Social Life of the Clans," in *The Highlands and the Highlanders*, ed. by the Highlands Committee for the Empire Exhibition, Scotland, 1938 (Glasgow, 1938), pp. 9 ff.

9. John Lorne Campbell, "The Gaelic Schools, 1818-1825," in *The Book of Barra*, ed. by John Lorne Campbell (London, 1936), pp. 87-97.

10. See the article "Bagpipes" in the *Encyclopaedia Britannica* (14th ed., 1929).

11. See John Alexander Duke, *The Columban Church* (Oxford, 1932); and for a much fuller background, G. F. Frank Knight, *Archaeological Light on the Early Christianizing of Scotland*, 2 vols. (London, 1933).

12. Joseph Anderson in his *Scotland in Early Christian Times* (Edinburgh, 1881), and *Scotland in Early Christian Times*, Second Series (Edinburgh, 1881), describes Celtic structural remains: relics such as books, bells, crosiers, reliquaries; decorative metal-work such as brooches; decorative stone-work and inscribed monuments. Examples of the weaver's art have perished entirely; see J. Romilly Allen, *Celtic Art in Pagan and Christian Times* (London, 1904), p. 129, and H. F. McClintock, *Old Irish and Highland Dress and That of the Isle of Man* (2nd ed., Dundalk, 1950). Scottish Gaelic music was not written down until the eighteenth century, but much of the traditional music orally preserved is very ancient, some examples being based on a pentatonic scale; see Annie G. Gilchrist, "Notes on the Modal System of Gaelic Tunes," *Journal of the Folk-Song Society*, London, vol. 4, no. 16 (Dec., 1911), pp. 150-3. Scottish Gaelic poetry was not written down until the sixteenth century, but its oral tradition is likewise of considerable age; see Magnus MacLean, *The Literature of the Celts* (London, 1902), pp. 115-33.

13. See Thomas Ratcliffe Barnett, *Margaret of Scotland, Queen and Saint* (Edinburgh and London, 1926).

14. *Regimen Sanitatis: A Gaelic Medical Manuscript of the Early Sixteenth Century from the Vade Mecum of the Famous MacBeaths, Physicians to the Lords of the Isles and the Kings of Scotland for Several Centuries*, ed. by H. Cameron Gillies (Glasgow, 1911).

15. The treatise remains unpublished. See Alexander Cameron, *Reliquiae Celticae*, vol. 2 (Inverness, 1894), p. 145.

16. Farquharson, quoted in *Sketch of Missionary Proceedings at Cape Breton from August 1833, to September 1836* (n.p., n.d.), pp. 16-17.

17. Alexander Carmichael reports that some cows would even refuse to give milk unless the milk-maid sang their favourite airs. See Carmichael, *Carmina*, vol. 1, p. 258.

18. Taken down from the recitation of Neil mac Lachlainn Chleves MacDonald of Albert Bridge, Cape Breton, in 1943. His grandfather came from North Uist. A similar rime set to music is recorded by Mrs. Marjory Kennedy-Fraser and the Reverend Kenneth MacLeod, *Songs of the Hebrides* (1909), vol. 1, p. 40.

19. Taken down from the recitation of Kenneth mac Eoghain Ferguson, St. Esprit, Cape Breton, in 1943. His ancestors came from Harris.

20. Taken down from the recitation of Mrs. Hugh Gillis, MacKinnon's Harbour, Cape Breton, in 1943.

21. Carmichael, *Carmina*, vol. 4, p. 96.

22. Taken down from the recitation of Neil MacDonald, already mentioned in note 18.

23. Taken down from the recitation of the late Joe N. MacKenzie of Christmas Island, Cape Breton, in 1943. His ancestors came from Barra; see MacKenzie, *History*, p. 57.

24. See, for instance, John Francis Campbell, *Popular Tales of the West Highlands* (new ed., Paisley and London, 1890-3), especially vol. 3. A partial list of collections of Scottish Gaelic folk-tales is included in Johannes Bolte and Georg Polivka, *Anmerkungen zu den Kinder- und Haus-märchen der Brüder Grimm* (Leipzig, 1932), vol. 5, p. 53.

25. The version here translated and synopsized was recorded in 1943 from the recitation of the late Joe N. MacKenzie mentioned in note 23. Its type is classified as Mt. 875 in Stith Thompson, *The Types of the Folk-Tale*, Folklore Fellows Communications, no. 74 (Helsinki, 1928). Subsequent to Thompson's list are further references in Folklore Fellows Communications nos. 78, 81, and 90 (under Mt. 875), and in no. 120 (under "Schwänke 28, Die klüge Frau, II and X").

26. Bishop John Carswell in the preface to his *Foirm na nUrrnuidheadh* (Edinburgh, 1567); as reprinted, *The Book of Common Order Commonly Called John Knox's Liturgy Translated into Gaelic by Mr. John Carswell*, ed. by Thomas M'Lauchlan (Edinburgh, 1873), p. 19.

27. Murray, *History*, p. 265.

28. Concerning second sight, forerunners, the evil eye, and the Witch of Mull, see Mary K. Fraser, *Folklore of Nova Scotia* (n.p., n.d.), pp. 32-51, 63-8.

29. Carmichael, *Carmina*, vol. 1, p. xxiii.

30. Examples of these may be found in vol. 3 of the collection by J. F. Campbell mentioned in note 24.

31. There are many variant versions of this popular song; the verses here quoted are from Fionn, *The Celtic Lyre* (Edinburgh, 1906), no. 11.

32. The various editions will be found enumerated incompletely in MacLean, *Typographia*, pp. 247-9.

33. *Mac-Talla*, vol. 9, no. 5 (Aug. 3, 1900), p. 35.

34. Taken down from the recitation of Neil (R. B.) MacKenzie, Christmas Island, Cape Breton, in 1943. His ancestors came from Barra; for his genealogy see MacKenzie, *History*, p. 57.

35. Taken down in 1943 from the recitation of William MacVicar, who is mentioned in ch. 3, note 17. His ancestors came from North Uist.

36. Taken down in 1943 from the recitation of Kenneth Ferguson, already mentioned in note 19.

37. See William Forbes Skene, *Celtic Scotland* (2nd ed., Edinburgh, 1890), vol. 3, pp. 336-8, 346-64.

38. Neil MacDonald, already mentioned in note 18.

39. The late Joe N. MacKenzie, already mentioned in note 23.

40. In a letter to the editor, *Mac-Talla*, vol. 3, no. 39, p. 1.

41. See MacDougall, *History*, p. 232.

42. Carmichael, *Carmina*, vol. 1, p. xxxii.

43. The Reverend George Patterson, *A History of the County of Pictou* (Montreal, 1877), pp. 80, 456.

44. From the reminiscences of an early settler quoted by Ada MacLeod, "The Glenaladale Pioneers," *Dalhousie Review*, vol. 11 (Oct. 1931), p. 317.

45. *Mac-Talla*, vol. 10, no. 26 (March 14, 1902), p. 197.

46. *Smeorach*, p. 6.

47. Dr. A. Gesner in R. C. MacDonald, *Sketches of Highlanders* (St. John, N.B., 1843), "Appendix," p. viii.

48. See Edward Dwelly, *The Illustrated Gaelic-English Dictionary* (4th ed., Glasgow, 1941), under "poit-dhubh," pp. 730-1.

Chapter 5 (pp. 58-73)

1. Rev. A. M. Sinclair, "Memoir of John MacLean," in *Clarsach*, pp. xiv-xxi.

2. From *Oran do dh' America* in *Clarsach*, pp. 90-4. *Clarsach* has *chruinn* in the third line quoted, but *chruim* is intended and may be found in the original in Dr. Hector MacLean's manuscript (now owned by George Maclean Sinclair, Hopewell, N.S.), folio 136; the phrase 's a' choille chruim* occurs again in the Bard's work in *Clarsach*, p. 128.

3. Published in *Dain Spioradail le Iain Mac-Gilleain*, ed. by the Reverend Alexander Maclean Sinclair (Edinburgh, 1880).

4. John Dochanassie Cameron, *Marbh-rann do'n Bhard MacGhilleathain*, in *Clarsach*, pp. 247-9.

5. See above, ch. 3, n. 8. In *The Gaelic Bards from 1715 to 1765*, ed. by the Reverend Alexander Maclean Sinclair (Charlottetown, P.E.I., 1892), p. 254, the date of MacRae's emigration should read 1774, not 1674.

6. Patterson, *Memoir*, pp. 448-55.

7. Both songs are written in a copy of Eoin Gillies, *Dain agus Orain Ghaidhealach* (Perth, 1786), bearing on the fly-leaf the signature "Seumas MacGriogair, 1791," and preserved in the library of the late Reverend Alexander Maclean Sinclair, at Hopewell, N.S., now in the possession of George Maclean Sinclair. *Rainn do MhacGriogair* is on p. 180 and was published in *Mac-Talla*, vol. 9, no. 30 (Jan. 25, 1901), p. 232. *Oran Gaoil* is on the fly-leaves and was published in *Clarsach*, pp. 231-3.

8. Details in Patterson, *Memoir*, pp. 298-308.

9. See *Gaelic Bards*, pp. 139-40.

10. In *Clarsach*, pp. 242-6.

11. From his *Braigh' Abhainn Bharnaidh* in *Gaelic Bards*, pp. 106-7.

12. From *Am Faigh a' Ghaidhlig Bas?* in Neil MacLeod, *Clarsach na Doire* (Edinburgh, 1883), p. 20.

13. In *Smeorach*, pp. 1-2.

14. See *Smeorach*, p. x, and *The Canadian-American Gael*, vol. 1 (Cape Breton Island ed., Sydney, N.S., 1943), p. 90.

15. From *Am Braighe*, already mentioned in note 13.

16. Subsequent quotations from *Oran* in *Smeorach*, pp. 8-10.

17. *Moladh a' Chuil agus Di-moladh a' Chladaich* in *Smeorach*, pp. 113-15; concerning MacDonald see *Smeorach*, p. x.

18. In *Moladh a' Chladaich agus Di-moladh a' Chuil* in *Smeorach*, pp. 110-12. Supplementary information supplied by D. D. MacFarlane, South-West Margaree, Cape Breton.

19. In an undated clipping from a Sydney, N.S., newspaper (probably around 1918).

20. In MacKenzie, *History*, pp. 166-7.

21. In *Mac-Talla*, vol. 11, no. 25 (June 12, 1903), p. 199; and, with one verse omitted, in *Smeorach*, pp. 126-7.

22. See MacDougall, *History*, pp. 205-6, 332.

23. Taken down in 1943 from the recitation of Mrs. John A. MacLean, Albert Bridge, Cape Breton; the composer, according to tradition, was Ewen MacQueen of Peter's Brook, Cape Breton.

24. In *Clarsach*, pp. 112-117.

25. Morrison, *Orain;* written down by D. K. Finlayson and published at the expense of the late Judge Alexander Finlayson, both of Grand River, Cape Breton.

26. *The Cape Breton Collection of Scottish Melodies for the Violin*, ed. by J. Beaton (Medford, Mass., 1940).

Chapter 6 (pp. 74-90)

1. See the Reverend Donald Maclean Sinclair, "Gaelic Newspapers and Prose Writings in Nova Scotia," *Collections of the Nova Scotia Historical Society*, vol. 26 (1945), pp. 105-13. The best collections of New World Gaelic literature are to be found in the Harvard College Library, Cambridge, Mass.; the St. Francis Xavier College Library, Antigonish, N.S.; and the private library of the late Reverend Alexander Maclean Sinclair, now in the possession of his son, George Maclean Sinclair, Hopewell, N.S.

2. *The Colonial Records of North Carolina*, ed. by William L. Saunders (Raleigh, N.C., 1890), vol. 10, p. 544.

3. Details in *Gaidheal*, Aug., 1872, p. 160; and in Hew Scott, *Fasti Ecclesiae Scoticanae* (new ed., Edinburgh, 1923), vol. 4, pp. 63, 65. Listed in MacLean, *Typographia*, pp. 102-3; this work may also be consulted regarding the other works mentioned in the present chapter.

4. MacLean, *Typographia*, p. 113.

5. Dughall Buchannan, *Laoidhean Spioradail*, and Paruig Grannd, *Dain Spiora-dail*, bound in one volume (Montreal, 1836). Not listed in MacLean, *Typographia*.

6. *Iul a' Chriostaidh* (Charlottetown, P.E.I., 1841). MacLean, *Typographia*, pp. 87-8, mentions later editions but not this one.

7. Details may be found concerning himself and his father, John the Piper, in the Reverend Ronald MacGillivray, "The County of Antigonish," ch. xi, in *Casket*, July 29, 1943, and ch. xx, in *Casket*, Sept. 16, 1943; in *The Glenbard Collection of Gaelic Poetry*, ed. by the Reverend Alexander Maclean Sinclair (Charlottetown, P.E.I., 1890), pt. 3, pp. 344, 393; in *Clarsach*, pp. 234-6; and in MacLean, *Typographia*.

8. W. Moorsom, *Letters from Nova Scotia* (London, 1830), p. 99.

9. Alastair McGillevra [= Alexander MacGillivray], *Companach an Oganaich, no An Comhairliche Taitneach* (Pictou, N.S., 1836), p. 105.

10. In *Companach*, mentioned in note 9, p. 56.

11. Listed in MacLean, *Typographia*.

12. Mentioned in *Mac-Talla*, vol. 2, no. 13 (Sept. 23, 1893) p. 3.

13. See the Reverend Ronald MacGillivray, "The County of Antigonish," ch. xix, in *Casket*, Sept. 16, 1943; and MacLean, *Typographia*. The two accounts conflict in some details; probably MacLean is at fault, as his information is not always reliable.

14. Reverend Ronald MacGillivray, ch. xix; see note 13.

15. *Casket*, vol. 1, no. 1 (June 24, 1852), supplement, p. 4.

16. *Casket*, vol. 1, no. 7 (Aug. 5, 1852), supplement, p. 28.

17. *Gaidheal*, vol. 1, no. 3, English supplement, p. 45.

18. See the "Memoir" by his son, the Reverend Donald Maclean Sinclair, in *Clarsach*, pp. xxii-xxiv; and two pamphlets by the Reverend Alexander Maclean Sinclair: *A Brief Genealogical Account of the MacLeans of Glenbard together with a Few Poems by Mary MacLean* (Charlottetown, P.E.I., 1891), and *The Sinclairs of Roslin, Caithness, and Goshen* (Charlottetown, P.E.I., 1901).

19. See *The MacLean Bards*, ed. by the Reverend Alexander Maclean Sinclair (Charlottetown, P.E.I., 1898), vol. 1, pp. 5-7.

20. See the bibliography of his work in *Clarsach*, p. xxiv; to this list should be added *The Gaelic Bards from 1825 to 1875* (Sydney, N.S., 1904).

21. Compare, for instance, the manuscript originals of two of the Bard's poems published in *Clarsach*, pp. 6-11, 14-19, with the edited versions in *Clarsach*, pp. 1-5, 11-13. But see his own remarks in *Clarsach*, pp. vi-vii, and Hector MacDougall's comments in *Clarsach*, pp. viii-ix.

22. In a postscript to *Dain agus Orain le Alasdair Mac-Fhionghain* (Charlottetown, P.E.I., 1902), pp. 41-8.

23. In *The Gaelic Bards from 1411 to 1517* [a misprint for 1715], ed. by the Reverend Alexander Maclean Sinclair (Charlottetown, P.E.I., 1890), p. 155.

24. *Clarsach*, p. xvii.

25. See *Mac-Talla*, vol. 1., no. 1 (May 28, 1892), p. 2. The editor's brother, Don MacKinnon of Sydney, also gave useful information.

26. *Mac-Talla*, vol. 3, no. 24, p. 4.

27. See *Mac-Talla*, vol. 12, no. 26 (June 24, 1904), p. 193.

28. *Mac-Talla*, vol. 7, no. 41 (May 12, 1899), p. 327; no. 42 (May 19, 1899), p. 335.

29. *Mac-Talla*, vol. 6, no. 5 (July 30, 1897), p. 33.

30. From an unpublished Gaelic song in manuscript at St. Francis Xavier University, Antigonish, N.S.

31. *Mac-Talla*, vol. 10, no. 17 (Nov. 1, 1901), p. 124.

32. See p. 126.

33. See account of an interview with the editor in John Lorne Campbell, "A Visit to Cape Breton," *Scots Magazine*, new series, no. 29 (Sept. 1938), pp. 423-32, and no. 30 (Oct., 1938), pp. 17-27.

34. *Mac-Talla*, vol. 12, no. 26 (June 24, 1904), p. 193.

35. In *Mac-Talla*, vol. 9, no. 12 (Sept. 21, 1900), p. 94, Malcolm Chisholm writes from Dawson and says that he hears more Gaelic there than he would in Strathglass, Scotland.

36. *Mac-Talla*, vol. 3, no. 48, p. 4.

37. *Mac-Talla*, vol. 10, no. 2 (July 12, 1901), p. 9.

38. *Am Piobaire Breac agus Da Sgeul Eile* (Sydney, N.S., 1919); *Far am Bi Gradh, Bidh Dia, le Count Leo Tolstoi* (Sydney, N.S., 1924); *An Triuir Choigreach, le Tomas*

Hardy (Sydney, N.S., n.d.); and *Sgeul an Draoidh Eile, le Eanruig Van Dyke* (Dunfermline, 1938).

39. Jonathan G. MacKinnon, *Old Sydney: Sketches of the Town and Its People in Days Gone By* (Sydney, N.S., 1918).

40. *Oran do Cheap Breatunn* in *Fear*, vol. 1, no. 11 (March, 1929), p. 88.

41. Published in the *Richmond County Record*, Arichat, N.S.

42. See *Casket*, April 1, 1926.

43. For information concerning him see *The Celtic Who's Who* (Kirkcaldy, Scotland, 1921), pp. 47-9, and *The Canadian Who's Who* (London and Toronto, 1910), vol. 1.

44. *Steelworker and Miner*, Sydney, N.S., Jan. 9, 1943.

45. In *Casket*, February 12, 1920. See ch. 2, note 9.

Chapter 7 (pp. 91-107)

1. John Sealgair MacDonald, *Oran do dh' America;* source already specified in ch. 2, note 29.

2. Ann Gillis, *Canada Ard*, in *Gaelic Bards*, pp. 7-8.

3. According to "Conal" in a letter dated Aug., 1893, at "An Camus" published in an unidentified newspaper, in *Clippings*, vol. 1, p. 129, col. 2.

4. Patterson, *Memoir*, pp. 311-14.

5. [Jonathan G. MacKinnon,] "Historical Notes," *Annual Report, 1931, The Parish of Whycocomagh, United Church of Canada* (Sydney, n.d.), p. 11.

6. See the Reverend Roderick MacKenzie, "Historical Sketch of Early Missions" in *Centenary*, and quoted in part in MacKenzie, *History*, pp. 3-7; and John A. MacDougall, "Brief Sketch of Christmas Island Parish" in *Centenary*, and quoted in part in MacKenzie, *History*, pp. 7-9.

7. Murray, *History*, p. 264.

8. *Mac-Talla*, vol. 11, no. 4 (Aug. 22, 1902), p. 31.

9. Archibald MacDonald, *Marbhrann d' a Mhnaoi*, in a collection of his poems, p. 3; the title-page was missing on the only copy I was able to find, but friends of the author suggested that the title was *Laoidhean Ghilleasbuig 'ic Dhomhnuill Oig an New Boston* (Sydney, 1901).

10. Quoted by his brother, the Reverend Donald MacLeod, in his *Memoir of Norman MacLeod, D.D.* [of the Barony], 2 vols. in 1 (New York, 1877), vol. 1, pp. 241-2.

11. Bibliographical details concerning the various works mentioned in this chapter may be found under the authors' names in MacLean, *Typographia*.

12. See Joseph Mainzer, *The Gaelic Psalm Tunes of Ross-shire* (Edinburgh, 1844).

13. See, for instance, the account of the church at Orwell Head, P.E.I., in Malcolm A. MacQueen, *Skye Pioneers and "The Island"* (Winnipeg, 1929), p. 65.

14. The Reverend Malcolm Campbell, *Cape Breton Worthies* (Sydney, 1913), pp. 3 ff.

15. Patterson, *Memoir*, pp. 98, 104, 217-18.

16. *Mac-Talla*, vol. 10, no. 11 (Sept. 13, 1901), p. 85.

17. The Reverend Norman MacLeod of the Barony makes the same observation about the Highlanders in Scotland in his *Reminiscences*, pp. 153-4.

18. John MacKay, "Reminiscences of a long Life: 1792-1884," pp. 12, 15; read by the Reverend Allan Pollock before the Nova Scotia Historical Society, May 2, 1913; typewritten copy preserved in the Public Archives of Nova Scotia, Halifax.

19. Isabel Frances Grant, *The Economic History of Scotland* (London, 1934), pp. 131-2.

20. Alexander the Ridge MacDonald in *Mac-Talla*, vol. 6, no. 52 (June 24, 1898), p. 416.

21. *Oran nan Gaidheal* in *Clarsach*, pp. 234-6. Concerning the author see ch. 6, note 7.

22. Quoted in Patterson, *Memoir*, p. 370.

23. Alexander D. MacLean, *The Washabuckt Pioneers and Some Incidents of the Early Days*, a typewritten pamphlet (Baddeck, N.S., 1936), pp. 28-9; Neil MacNeil, *The Highland Heart in Nova Scotia* (New York, 1948), pp. 78-9.

24. Judge John George Marshall, *Personal Narratives* (Halifax, N.S., 1866), p. 68.

Chapter 8 (pp. 108-22)

1. Compare with their situation the similar plight of the country people in the Highlands and Islands of Scotland when the gentry no longer mingled among them but preferred to live in the centres of fashion; this change is alluded to by Norman MacLeod of St. Columba's in *Caraid*, pp. 398-9 (translated incompletely by the Reverend Archibald Clerk in MacLeod, *Reminiscences*, p. 346).

2. John Howison, *Sketches of Upper Canada* (3rd ed., Edinburgh, 1825), p. 35.

3. Quoted in James S. Martell, *The Achievements of Agricola and the Agricultural Societies*, 1818-1825, Bulletin of the Public Archives of Nova Scotia, vol. 2, no. 2 (Halifax, N.S., 1940), p. 17.

4. W. Moorsom, *Letters from Nova Scotia* (London, 1830), p. 344.

5. Malcolm A. MacQueen, *Skye Pioneers and "The Island"* (Winnipeg, 1929), p. 26.

6. The father of Alexander MacGillivray; see ch. 6, note 7. This tradition was reported in conversation in Antigonish, 1943.

7. See the Reverend A. M. Sinclair's "Memoir" in *Clarsach*, p. xvii.

8. As recorded by the Reverend D. J. Rankin in an appendix to R. Gillis, *Stray Leaves from Highland History* (Sydney, 1918), pp. 35-6.

9. Morrison, *Orain*, p. 46.

10. Quoted in Patterson, *Memoir*, p. 106.

11. From *Craobhsgaoileadh a' Bhiobull agus an t-Soisgeul* in the Reverend James MacGregor, *Dain a Chomhnadh Crabhuidh* (Pictou, N.S., 1863), pp. 108-9.

12. Patterson, *Memoir*, p. 106.

13. Source specified in note 11.

14. MacLeod, *Reminiscences*, p. 133.

15. From the period of Samuel Johnson's *Journey* in 1773 right down to such recent works as Alexander McKechnie, *Introduction to Gaelic Scotland* (London and Glasgow, 1934), travellers have felt free to portray the bad characteristics of the Highlander, but they all agree, either grudgingly or willingly, about his independence of character.

16. MacLeod, *Reminiscences*, p. 138.

17. Murray, *History*, p. 181.

18. From *Oran do Innleachdan an Fheoir* in *Failte Cheap Breatuin*, ed. by Vincent A. MacLellan (Sydney, N.S., 1891), pp. 132-3.

19. From *Am ar n-Oige* in *Teachdaire nan Gaidheal*, vol. 5, no. 8 (July, 1933), p. 4 (composed in 1926).

20. In Morrison, *Orain*, p. 40.

21. In 1871 the population of Whycocomagh North was 1,865; *Eighth Census of Canada, 1941* (Ottawa, 1944), vol. 2, table 10.

22. Hutchinson, *Directory*, p. 378.

23. David McAlpine, *Nova Scotia Directory for 1868-1869* (Halifax, N.S., n.d.), pp. 818-19.

24. Hutchinson, *Directory*, p. 461.

25. Noted by Senex, "Old St. Andrew's," ch. vii, in *Casket*, Oct. 15, 1942; his figures are derived from Hutchinson, *Directory*.

26. Quoted in Patterson, *Memoir*, p. 369.

27. See, for instance, the writings of the leaders of the co-operative movement in Nova Scotia, such as the Reverend M. M. Coady, *Masters of Their Own Destiny* (2nd ed., New York and London, 1939), and George Boyle, *Democracy's Second Chance: Land, Work and Co-operation* (New York, 1941).

Chapter 9 (pp. 123-35)

1. The late Marcus L. Hansen in *The Mingling of the Canadian and American Peoples* (New Haven, Conn., 1939), vol. 1, presents a clear picture of the details of the mass migration from the rural eastern Maritimes to urban New England.

2. George S. MacDonald, "The Literary Aspect of the Keltic Settlement in the Counties of Stormont and Glengarry," *Transactions of the Celtic Society of Montreal* (Montreal, 1887), pp. 122-33.

3. Details gathered from MacKenzie, *History*, pp. 55-61.

4. *Eighth Census of Canada, 1941* (Ottawa, 1944) vol. 2, table 10. Those who know the individual areas in question may be surprised that the figures are as large as they

are, but it must be remembered that the census subdivisions include a larger territory than the post office areas.

5. Maximum in 1871 for Whycocomagh with 1,865 and North River with 929; maximum in 1891 for Little Narrows North and South with 899.

6. From *Gaidheal air Aineol* in MacKenzie, *History*, p. 165.

7. From *Gleann na Maiseadh* in MacKenzie, *History*, p. 164.

8. Details in MacKenzie, *History*, p. 114.

9. In *Casket*, Dec. 25, 1930, p. 8.

10. See *Smeorach*, p. xi.

11. In a song, *Cumha*, in *Smeorach*, p. 123.

12. *Aisling a' Mheinneadair Ghaidhealach* in *Casket*, Feb. 15, 1922, p. 2.

13. *A' Chailin Luachmhor* in *Mac-Talla*, vol. 6, no. 4 (July 23, 1897), p. 32, and republished in *Smeorach*, pp. 86-87.

14. *Mac-Talla*, vol. 3, no. 8 (Aug. 25, 1894), p. 8.

15. In an unpublished song composed for the Gaelic College at St. Ann's.

Chapter 10 (pp. 136-49)

1. "Name of MacLeod Much in Evidence," *Halifax Herald*, Halifax, N.S., Oct. 20, 1942.

2. According to Judge George Patterson, "The Coming of the 'Hector,' " *Studies in Nova Scotian History* (Halifax, N.S., 1940), p. 15.

3. See MacKenzie, *History*, pp. 81 ff., and *Fear*, vol. 1, no. 3 (May, 1928), pp. 21-3.

4. See *Gaelic Bards*, p. 38.

5. W. M'K., "Highland Emigrations in the Eighteenth Century," an undated clipping from unidentified newspaper, *Clippings*, vol. 3, p. 377.

6. See *Gaidheal*, June, 1872, p. 97; and *Mac-Talla*, vol. 2, no. 34, p. 5.

7. MacKenzie, *History*, p. 10.

8. Information obtained from the Reverend A. D. MacKinnon, Little Narrows, Cape Breton.

9. The Reverend J. D. Nelson MacDonald, Baddeck Forks, Cape Breton, in a letter dated Oct. 22, 1942.

10. See the history of these words in *A New English Dictionary on Historical Principles*, ed. by Sir J. A. H. Murray and others, 13 vols. (corrected reissue, Oxford, 1933).

11. See "Vocabulary of Rare and New Words" in [James MacNeil,] *Gaelic Lessons for Beginners* (Sydney, N.S., 1939), pp. 66-72.

12. Published in part in the volume mentioned in the previous note, p. 54.

13. See *Journal of Education*, Halifax, N.S., Sept., 1939, p. 863.

14. See *Annual Report of the Department of Education for . . . 1950* (Halifax, N.S., 1951), pp. xxvi, 169-70.

15. Dan Alec MacDonald's *Oran do Cheap Breatunn*, in *Teachdaire nan Gaidheal*, vol. 6, no. 12 (Feb., 1934), p. 5.

Chapter 11 (pp. 150-61)

1. From his *Oran do Cheap Breatunn*, referred to in ch. 6, note 40.

2. From his *Gleann na Maiseadh*, referred to in ch. 9, note 7.

3. In his "Eilean Cheap Breatunn," an unpublished song.

4. In *The Register of the Privy Council of Scotland*, ed. by David Masson (Edinburgh, 1889), vol. 9, p. 27. For a discussion of the background of the statutes, see Donald Gregory, *The History of the Highlands and Isles of Scotland from 1493 to 1625* (2nd ed., London, 1881), pp. 330 ff.

5. From his *Oran do Cheap Breatunn*, in *Smeorach*, p. 4.

6. *Oran do Bheinn Chlann-Domhnuill*, in *Failte Cheap Breatuin*, ed. by Vincent A. MacLellan, as reissued in typewritten form with additions, ed. by James H. MacNeil (Sydney, N.S., 1933), pp. 231-3.

Index